'olley's
Cc oration Tax

Post-Budget Supplement

by

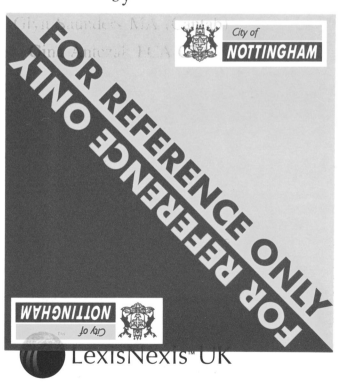

LexisNexis UK

About This Supplement

This post-Budget supplement gives details of changes in the law and practice of corporation tax from the publication of Tolley's Corporation Tax 2002/03 to 9 April 2003, immediately before the Chancellor's Budget speech on that day. It lists the changes in the same order and under the same paragraph headings as in the 2002/03 edition. It also includes a summary of the Budget proposals announced on 9 April 2003.

Each time the 2002/03 edition of Tolley's Corporation Tax is used, reference should also be made to the material contained in this supplement. The *Contents* gives a list of all the chapters and paragraphs which have been updated.

TOLLEY

Contents

This supplement contains amendments to the chapters and paragraphs of Tolley's Corporation Tax 2002/03 as listed below. There is also a summary of the 9 April 2003 Budget proposals.

Contents

Contents

1 Introduction and Rates of Tax

1.1 **General.** The following note is added.

'The Government published on 5 August 2002 a consultation document "Reform of corporation tax" seeking views on three potential areas for reform of the corporate tax system:

(*a*)   the tax treatment of capital assets not covered by earlier reforms;

(*b*)   rationalisation of the way in which the schedular system taxes various types of income; and

(*c*)   the differences in the tax treatment of trading and investment companies.

The document is available on both the Revenue and the Treasury websites.'

4 Anti-Avoidance

4.3 **Treasury consents — transfer etc. of securities to non-residents.** It is noted that the address for applications for Treasury consent, and for notification of certain movements of capital, is now Mark Ritchie, Revenue Policy, International, Business Tax Group (Treasury Consent), Victory House, 30–34 Kingsway, London WC2B 6ES.

4.4 **Transfer pricing: accounting periods ending before 1 July 1999.** A reference is added to an article in the Revenue Tax Bulletin (February 2003 pp 1002–1007), reproduced below, on the application of the transfer pricing rules to employee share scheme costs, in particular in relation to a recent decision of the Special Commissioners.

'SHARE OPTIONS AND AWARDS AND TRANSFER PRICING: WATERLOO PLC, EUSTON & PADDINGTON V CIR (SPC 301) ("WATERLOO")

This article sets out the Revenue's view on the application of transfer pricing principles to share option and share award schemes following a recent Special Commissioners' decision on this subject and the publication on 19 December 2002 of the draft legislation relating to the new statutory corporation tax deduction for employee acquisitions.

The new statutory deduction will be available to a company within the charge to corporation tax for accounting periods beginning on or after 1 January 2003, where an employee of that company acquires shares in that or another company whose shares meet the requirements for relief. The deduction will be equivalent to the difference between the market value of the shares at the time they are acquired and the amount payable by the recipient, or another, in respect of the shares. No other deduction will be allowed for corporation tax purposes in respect of the cost of providing the shares. The draft legislation and a technical commentary are available on the Inland Revenue website at http://home.inrev.uk/bud2003/pbr/documents/2021217.

One result of the draft legislation is to override the requirement in certain circumstances for taxpayers to consider whether schedule 28AA ICTA 1988 requires a transfer pricing adjustment. For accounting periods beginning on or after 1 January 2003, where employees of a UK company acquire shares in a non UK affiliate by reason of their employment **and** the UK company is able to obtain the statutory deduction the transfer pricing legislation is otiose because whatever amount is recharged in the accounts will be disallowed by the new legislation.

Where a statutory deduction is not available, for example, because the shares are not of a qualifying type or the accounting period begins before 1 January 2003 the relevant transfer pricing legislation will apply and any corporation tax deduction must be based on arms length principles. The transfer pricing legislation will continue to apply to all accounting periods, whether starting before, on or after 1 January 2003, in respect of the cost to UK companies of providing shares for employees of non-UK affiliates. This is because the statutory deduction only applies where shares are acquired by reason of employment with a UK company and the costs will not otherwise be incurred for the purposes of the UK company's business. Transfer pricing legislation will also apply to expenses incurred by a UK company in establishing, administering or borrowing for the purposes of an employee share scheme (which are not affected by the statutory deduction) where that scheme provides shares for employees of non-UK affiliates.

Where transfer pricing legislation does apply to the costs of providing share options, as set out above, then the Revenue's approach will be based on its interpretation of a recent Special Commissioners decision concerning the application of the transfer pricing legislation to such share option schemes.

The case considered by the Special Commissioners involved a UK company, Waterloo, which allowed employees of non-UK subsidiaries to participate in its share schemes. The decision also clarifies a number of issues arising in the reverse situation – where UK subsidiaries are charged by non UK parent companies in respect of options granted to UK based employees. Prior to the Special Commissioners' decision, there was no generally prevailing practice as to how to establish the arm's length price of share options granted by a parent company to the employees of a subsidiary. In accordance with the principles set out in TB44D (generally prevailing practice) the Revenue regards the Special Commissioners decision as applying to earlier periods, subject to the statutory time limits for making assessments and opening enquiries, and the normal rules governing discovery.

There may, however, be a considerable period between the grant of an option and its exercise. Accordingly the Revenue will not seek to apply the Waterloo decision in place of whatever approach has been used in the computations in respect of deductions claimed for options exercised in accounting periods ended before 1 January 1997 except in exceptional circumstances. These circumstances will be, for example, where there are open transfer pricing enquiries (not necessarily explicitly about share options) for the earlier periods; or where enquiries into deductions for share options had been opened (for any period) prior to publication of the Special Commissioners' decision; or where such enquiries had been closed following the provision of misleading information by the company.

Where companies have in periods starting before 1 January 2003 claimed an amount based on the spread at the date of exercise, the transitional rules will not be relevant. This is because options which have been exercised no longer exist at the commencement of the new legislation, so no statutory deduction can be due for such options. Where, on the other hand, companies have made deductions in respect of unexercised options in accounts for periods beginning before 1 January 2003 the transitional rules will apply. In such circumstances a deduction will be allowed for the arms length price in the appropriate period pre 1 January 2003. When the options are exercised (or shares acquired) by the employee, the statutory deduction will be available, reduced by the arms length amount(s) allowed in earlier periods. This might reduce the new relief to nil but does not create a charge to tax if the earlier amounts exceed the statutory deduction.

Waterloo plc etc

Facts

Waterloo established a trust in connection with its employee share option scheme and made an interest free loan to the trustees so that they could purchase shares and grant options in respect of those shares to employees of Waterloo's subsidiaries. When options were exercised the employees paid the option price to the trustees who then repaid the loan. Waterloo also undertook to issue shares to the trustees at the option price so that options could be satisfied in the event that the trustees exhausted their reserve of shares.

Point At Issue

Whether business facilities were provided within the meaning of s773(4) ICTA 88.

Decision

The Commissioners found that there was a business facility which "was more than the grant of interest free loans by Waterloo to the trustee; what Waterloo gave was the total facility for giving benefits to employees in the form of options". (para 51). Waterloo devised, set up, funded and operated a facility whereby the employees of its subsidiary companies were able to receive valuable share options. The facility was not just the making of the interest free loan, nor was it just the selling of shares to employees at a price below market value. The facility was the total package and it is the total package that needs to be examined and priced. The distinction between the "total facility" and the constituent transactions such as the loan is important and has implications beyond share options though these are not the subjects of this article. It is consistent with the Revenue's submission that "the phrase "business facility" is a commercial not a legal term, and … that where a commercial term is used in legislation, the test of ordinary business might require an aggregation of transactions which transcended their juristic individuality" (para 57).

Waterloo concerned the award of shares by way of options but the principles are clearly applicable to any share based remuneration scheme. The relevant transfer pricing legislation for the years covered by the appeals was s770 ICTA 1988, which was replaced by schedule 28AA ICTA 88 for periods ending after 1 July 1999. The Revenue regards schedule 28AA as being of wider application than s770 so will be applying the decision to periods ending after 1 July 1999 as well as periods for which s770 ICTA 1988 applied.

The Arms length Price

Although not asked to consider pricing, the Special Commissioners commented that "it would be relatively simple" to price the facility by reference to the costs of the provider of the facility; and went on to enumerate the types of costs to be included (para 102). The Revenue takes the view that the Commissioners would have been extremely unlikely to endorse pricing by reference to the employee's gain on exercise (the difference between the market value at the date of exercise and the exercise price – known as "the spread"). This is because the costs of Waterloo were related largely to interest rates not to the increase in share price over the period of the option.

Where Waterloo issued new shares there is an argument that, under accountancy standards applicable in the years of the appeals, the company did not incur a cost. Arguably no charge should be made. It might appear on such reasoning that where a non-UK company issues shares in support of options granted to employees of its UK subsidiaries then the full amount of any charge made to the subsidiaries would be disallowed. However, parties acting at arm's length are prepared to pay for something of value to them even if there is no cost to the provider. Indeed, the Special Commissioners allude to one example elsewhere in the decision when they accepted the giving of bank guarantees as the provision of a business facility (para 52).

The Revenue approach

Any enterprise which grants share options does so in the expectation that the value of the shares will rise. A prudent business would look to hedge in some way the exposure to the expected share price increases. This presumption is borne out by the difficulty in finding groups that wait till options are exercised before buying shares in the market, thereby exposing themselves to increases in the share price. It is sometimes argued that, since share price increases are linked to profit increases, there is no need for the prudent business to hedge actively – the correlation between share prices and profits supposedly providing its own natural hedge. If this proposition were valid – and the difficulty of finding groups who have acted upon it suggest otherwise – then any correlation that exists between share price and profits would be stronger at a group consolidated level than at the level of the individual operating entity. It follows that if the group as a whole adopts an active hedging strategy of some sort then so should the subsidiary, which does not have the same correlation between its stand-alone profits and the group's share price.

Using group policy in this way as a starting point for the subsidiary's policy is in line with OECD guidance on group hedging strategies for dealing with foreign exchange or interest rate exposures which states:

> "When addressing the issue of the extent to which a party to a transaction bears any …risk, it will normally be necessary to consider the extent, if any, to which the taxpayer and/or the MNE group have a business strategy which deals with the minimisation or management of such risks" (OECD 1995 1.27)

Where exceptionally the group as a whole does not have a hedging strategy, the Revenue will consider whether the same unhedged strategy is appropriate for the subsidiary, bearing in mind that individual entities may not have the same correlation between profits and the group's share price as the group as a whole has.

There are 3 hedging strategies open to a company granting options to employees over its shares:

a.   issue new shares

b.   buy shares in the market at or around the time options are granted

c.   buy an option that mirrors the terms of the options granted to the employees

Subsidiaries, whose employees are granted options over the parent company's shares, cannot use option a. Similarly, a company granting options over its own shares is unlikely to opt for c. However, option c. approximates to how a subsidiary could hedge its exposure if it did not buy shares in the market; and one measure of the amount a party acting at arm's length would be prepared to pay is the cost of obtaining the same benefit by a different route. This article considers the application of pricing by reference to options b. and c.

Shares bought in the market (Market Purchase Price)

Where shares are bought in the market the Special Commissioners found that the facility was not simply the making of a loan. Pricing the facility is not therefore simply a matter of pricing the loan. Rather the pricing of the loan is one ingredient in establishing the price of the facility. In the Waterloo case there was not an exact match between the exercise price of the option and the price of the shares acquired for hedging. Instead shares were purchased during the year at propitious times in anticipation of the grant of options later, so the price of the shares could be more or less than the exercise price of the option. Other groups may buy some shares before the grant of options and some after. Provided the parent company does not have an ulterior motive (such as supporting its share price) the actual purchase pattern of the parent is a good starting point for determining an appropriate strategy for the subsidiary.

Table 1 sets out how a UK headed group might calculate the charge to its non UK affiliates for options granted to employees of those affiliates. For the sake of simplicity the example assumes that options are granted at the year end and the mid year point is when options are exercised and shares purchased in advance of the next tranche of options. The example also assumes that the costs of acquiring more shares than are required for hedging are costs of the parent company, and are not to be allocated to the subsidiaries. Thus the allocation of non UK costs are determined by the ratio of non UK shares needed (C) to total shares needed (and not non UK shares needed to shares held). In practice how the costs of "excess" share purchases are allocated will depend on the precise circumstances. If the parent company routinely and persistently over purchases it may be that it is doing so for its own purposes.

If, on the other hand, it is sometimes over and sometimes under it may be that this is a valid hedging strategy for the share option awards so that all costs are allocable.

Expected rate of exercise – if, historically, only say 60% of options granted were actually exercised, one would expect a prudent business to purchase 60 shares for every 100 options granted. Expected rates of exercise may vary from group to group depending on such factors as staff turnover and performance conditions attaching to the options. For new schemes documentation about expected take up may have been produced internally or by remuneration consultants involved in setting up the scheme. Such documentation could form the basis of expected rates of exercise until more reliable data is available.

Rate of interest – as with any loan the arm's length rate of interest depends upon the facts and circumstances of the case. Interest is calculated from the date the shares are purchased, not the date the options are granted.

Dividends – typically dividends are waived on shares held by share scheme trusts so that dividends payable to other shareholders are not diluted. A subsidiary acquiring shares from a hypothetical third party for its employees would not care about the interest of the other shareholders. The only concern would be with minimising the costs of its hedging strategy. So in calculating the price of an arms length hedging strategy there would be no reason to waive the dividends.

Profits and losses on disposal of shares – the example at Table 1 does not include an explicit entry for profits or losses that might arise on the disposal of shares. Such profits and losses are, however, included implicitly in the calculation since disposal proceeds on the sale of shares affect the amount of debt left in the trust, which in turn determines the amount of interest to be allocated to the subsidiaries. Share option schemes tend to be enduring structures and one might expect profits and losses to balance out sufficiently over the life of the scheme so that all debt is repaid : shares purchased to hedge a tranche of options which lapse while the options are under the water become the hedge for a second tranche of options granted when the share price recovers. In a period of steep and prolonged decline in share prices, however, it may be that the group decides to sell surplus shares to prevent further losses arising. The losses incurred on selling surplus shares may be so great that part of the loan to the trust will never be repaid. In such circumstances it may be appropriate to include as an ingredient in the price of the facility an amount for loans permanently written off. Such an apportionment might not be straightforward. The objectives and actual pattern of disposal of surplus shares of the parent company (whose shares are held in the trust) may be different to the pattern of disposal that would have been chosen by a subsidiary whose only interest in the shares is as a hedge against its employee options.

Purchase of an option mirroring terms of options granted to employees

Another way to establish an arm's length price would be to calculate how much it would cost the subsidiary to purchase an option that mirrors the terms of the options granted to the employees (though legally such a transaction with the parent may not be permitted). Economic models such as Black-Scholes are used to value options and depend on a number of variables – volatility of shares, interest rates, dividend flows, maturity of options, etc. Such variables, moreover, may change over time. The Revenue understands that generally the price will be in the region of 25–35% of the value of the shares at time the option is granted but for nil-cost options could rise to 55–65%.

A hedging strategy priced on buying an option that mirrors the terms of the options granted to the employees should take account of the expected exercise rates. Again, if 60% of employees are expected to exercise the subsidiary employer would only require an option over a reduced number of shares. The fair value of the option would be spread over the vesting period of the employees' share options.

When applying models such as Black-Scholes, companies should bear in mind that they were not primarily designed for pricing options with the long maturity dates typical of employee share options. As such, substantial adjustments must be made to the model with the result that it is not as accurate as it might otherwise be. Therefore companies using Black-Scholes as their primary pricing method may want to check the result using a market purchase price.

For companies without in-house expertise in pricing options pricing by reference to buying the shares in the market may be simpler than using Black-Scholes. Accordingly, even where the scheme is actually hedged by the issue of shares rather than buying them in the market, the Revenue is prepared to accept a market purchase price, calculated along the lines of Tables 1; but assuming that the shares were purchased on the same day as the options were granted. However, and as indicated above, the share purchase model can become complicated where loans need to be written off and could become very difficult to apply when there are no actual loans or share disposal patterns to work from.

Treatment of Receipts by UK Parent

As indicated above, where shares are bought in the market the facility is not the making of an interest free loan and any receipt by the UK parent would be payment for a business facility, not interest. Similarly, inclusion of fair value of the options at grant in the price of the facility does not mean that the provider of the facility has actually sold an option to the trust (or subsidiary) mirroring the terms of the options granted to employees. Rather the price of such an option is merely an ingredient in pricing the facility. Where the parent, as in Waterloo, supports the scheme by a combination of market purchased and newly issued shares any payment received cannot – in light of the Commissioners finding of what the facility was – be separated out into capital and revenue. The receipt is indivisibly on revenue account and taxable as income.

When groups adopt structures that dispense with the trust and interest free loans and issue shares directly to the employees when they exercise the options then there may be no transfer pricing issue. At arms length one would still expect a third party to pay the issuing company, but provided the issuing company has not obtained a P&L deduction in respect of the option any receipt is likely to represent an increase in capital account and would not be caught by transfer pricing.

The issues arising on the quantum and nature of receipts in respect of share option schemes are unaffected by the proposed legislation giving a CT deduction for share options.

Treatment of payments by UK subsidiaries

Accounting periods starting before 1 January 2003

Following the Waterloo decision the Revenue will accept that an intra-group recharge paid by a UK subsidiary in respect of share options granted to its employees is allowable as a deduction for the period for which the recharge is made, if it is calculated on an arm's length basis as set out in this article and relates to employees who work exclusively for UK entities.

The Commissioners' analysis of the nature of the facility provided by the parent company in the Waterloo case means that the recharge is not capital expenditure and will be wholly and exclusively for the purposes of the subsidiary's trade if it relates to employees who work exclusively for it (Section 74(1) ICTA 1988). As the recharge is not a payment of emoluments or potential emoluments, but is payment for "the total facility for giving benefits to employees in the form of share options", Section 43 FA 1989 will not apply to defer the timing of any deduction.

Accounting periods starting on or after 1 January 2003

If the shares concerned are within the scope of the proposed new statutory deduction for the costs of providing shares for employee share schemes, the new legislation will determine the timing and amount of any deductions for providing shares to employees of UK companies.

To the extent that the new legislation does not disallow ancillary costs (such as interest on loans to purchase shares in the market) Schedule 28AA may still apply to recover such costs from non UK affiliates whose employees benefit from the scheme.

Cost Plus and Cost Sharing Arrangements

Pricing share options by reference to the gain made by the employee will not give the same result as applying general transfer pricing rules. It follows that transfer pricing methods which incorporate or rely upon profit made by the employee will not result in an arm's length price. Where, for example, a company is remunerated by affiliates on a cost plus basis, and those costs include a charge for share options based on the employee profit, the mark up has been applied to a non arm's length cost base. Similarly, where companies enter into cost sharing arrangements, and the costs include a charge for share options based on the employees' profit, the resulting sharing of costs will not be on an arm's length basis because a non arm's length cost was included in the pool. Cost Plus and Cost Sharing Arrangements must instead be based on an arm's length cost calculated according to one of the acceptable methods explained above. This will remain the case from 1 January 2003.

Summary

The Special Commissioners' decision has established that where a parent company allows the employees of its subsidiaries to participate in its share schemes, the arm's length principle requires that the subsidiaries make a contribution to the parent. The pricing of the facility is relatively straightforward for share award schemes (which are easier to value than options) and share options where the scheme is supported by purchasing shares in the market. The position is less clear cut where an option scheme is supported by the issue of new shares. Where new issue shares are used, the Revenues' view is that the fair value of the options at the date of grant, spread over the vesting period, is an appropriate arm's length price. As this could result in complex (and costly) calculations, pricing the facility as if it had been supported by market purchase of shares may also be acceptable.

Unless the group as a whole buys shares in the market at the date of exercise, charges based on the increase in market value of the shares over the vesting period are not arm's length, whether the charge is made at yearly rests or taken in full in the year of exercise.

The arms length principle will apply to the costs of all options exercised in accounting periods other than those starting on or after 1 January 2003. In addition the arms length principle will apply to the cost of options or other share awards or costs in connection with such awards when no statutory deduction is available on exercise in accounting periods starting on or after 1 January 2003.

Options	Year 1	Year 2	Year 3	Year 4	Year 5
Options b/f	0	1000	1100	850	850
Options granted	1000	600	0	0	150
price granted	1.75	2.5	0	0	3
Options exercised	0	500	250	0	300
options unexercised	1000	1100	850	850	700
Shares					
Non-UK Options	400	550	350	350	300
Exercise Rate	75%	75%	75%	75%	75%

Shares		Year 1	Year 2	Year 3	Year 4	Year 5
Shares needed non-UK **(C)**		300	413	263	263	225
Shares needed by trust **(D)**		750	825	638	638	525
Shares held by trust		900	1100	850	700	600
Loans						
opening loan	**(A)**	0	1485	2010	1573	1348
Shares Acquired		900	700	0	0	200
price		1.65	2			2.9
New Loan		1485	1400	0	0	580
shares sold		0	500	250	150	300
price			1.75	1.75	1.5	2.5
loan repaid		0	875	438	225	750
loan end of year	**(B)**	1485	2010	1573	1348	1178
rate of interest		5%	5%	5%	5%	5%
interest (A + B)/2		37	87	90	73	63
less div income		5	5	5	5	5
net cost	**(E)**	32	82	85	68	58
Non-UK =	**E × C/D**	13	41	35	28	25

Richard Gallacher
Revenue Policy International
Victory House
30-34 Kingsway
London
WC2B 6ES

Tel. 0207 438 6309

e-mail Richard.Gallacher@ir.gsi.gov.uk'

Transfer pricing: accounting periods ending on or after 1 July 1999. A reference is added to an article in the Revenue Tax Bulletin (August 2002 pp 943–947), reproduced below, giving guidance on the nature of the risk assessment carried out by the Revenue before undertaking a transfer pricing enquiry and a suggested timetabling framework for such enquiries.

'REVIEW OF LINKS WITH BUSINESS – INTERNATIONAL TAX ISSUES

The Review of links with business, published in November 2001, recommended (R35) that the Revenue should publish guidance that would:

- Better focus transfer pricing enquiries by giving more advice on the nature of the risk assessment to be carried out before the decision to embark on an enquiry is made.

- Facilitate the timetabling of the course of an enquiry, by setting out what could reasonably be expected of each side in terms of the time to provide information and to examine what is provided.

This article is concerned with transfer pricing enquiries into an enterprise's fundamental pricing structure for cross-border transactions with associated enterprises. These include enquiries into such areas as royalty rates, distributor margins, manufacturer margins, pricing methodologies (for example cost plus versus profit split). This article is not concerned with enquiries into such areas as thin capitalisation, imputation of interest on outward loans; guarantee fees, or management fees where such an area is the only cross border transaction. Such enquiries do not generally require the level of analysis of other transfer-pricing enquiries and do not normally take as long.

Representations received by the Revenue clearly favoured a collaborative approach to timetabling rather than a prescriptive or inflexible approach. This article sets out a collaborative approach. It is hoped that this will meet the best interests of both companies and the Revenue. Where it is not possible to pursue a collaborative approach enquiries will need to be based on what is specifically provided for in UK legislation supplemented by exchange of information powers in tax treaties. Such an approach is likely to be longer and less flexible than collaboration.

This article addresses Recommendation 35. It does not address Recommendation 34 (Transfer Pricing documentation requirements). However, the Revenue recognises that some taxpayers are anxious to know the level of documentation to be submitted with a CTSA return. In that context, we can reaffirm that, although there is a requirement that appropriate documentation needs to exist at the time the return is made, there is no requirement to provide such documentation as a routine matter along with a CTSA return.

Risk Assessment Process

Transfer pricing enquiries can be enormously resource intensive for both companies and the Revenue, so a transfer pricing enquiry should not be contemplated without first undertaking a detailed risk assessment.

In view of the potential resource cost of a full enquiry, transfer pricing risk assessments should be conducted to a greater level of detail than risk assessments in many other potential enquiry areas.

It is recommended that risk assessment should ideally include:

- A review of any previous transfer pricing papers
- A detailed examination of six years' consolidated group accounts and of accounts of individual UK and appropriate non-UK entities
- Consideration of the group structure and identification of haven/shelter countries
- A review of industry trends, details of the company's place in its sector, and recent developments within the group (new acquisitions, new locations, etc)
- A review of databases for multiple year data and potential comparables
- A review of company returns in other jurisdictions
- Liaison with PAYE office for details of highly-paid UK staff
- Possibly liaison with Customs & Excise

If such pre-enquiry work seems excessive in a particular case this may be an indication either that the case is not suitable for a transfer-pricing enquiry, or that any enquiry should have limited scope.

The mere presence of cross-border transactions between associated entities is not in itself sufficient reason to initiate a transfer-pricing enquiry, even if the amounts involved in the transactions are substantial. For example, a car distributor may purchase £1bn of cars from its foreign parent company, but if a net profit in line with commercial experience in car distribution is achieved on UK activities, there may be no substantial transfer pricing risk.

Obtaining Information for Risk Assessment

There may be difficulties obtaining some of the information outlined above; particularly with foreign owned small or medium sized groups. Such cases sometimes are not (even on a world-wide basis) large enough to feature on data bases, websites, sector commentaries, etc.

If the group as a whole does not feature in the above sources, this may be an indication that the UK operation is small: the potential tax at risk may not justify the resource cost of a transfer pricing enquiry for either the Revenue or the business.

In a large multi-national enterprise (MNE) the high value-adding activities can be located in any part of the group. There is a risk that UK companies within the group might be rewarded as if they were performing routine functions with low added value that understate the economic reality. With smaller firms, the high value-adding parts of the enterprise are more likely to be found in the home territory and this should be borne in mind when conducting risk assessments. Of course if the evidence of the accounts (e.g. large bonuses to staff) or other sources suggests otherwise then a different view of the risk may need to be taken.

Depending on the functions and role of the UK business, it may not always be necessary to know a lot about the rest of the group. For example if the UK business is a distributor, it may be appropriate to establish the arm's length price by examination of comparable uncontrolled transactions of independent UK distributors which would not necessarily involve analysing the results of the world-wide group.

Exchange of Information

Information powers under domestic UK law are not suitable for dealing with information not in a UK resident's power and possession.

UK subsidiaries can often legitimately say that some of the information requested in transfer pricing enquiries is in the power and possession only of a foreign associate. Where a double tax treaty with the UK exists and contains an Exchange of Information article, the UK Competent Authority can request the information about associated entities via his/her opposite number in the associate company's territory.

In the light of this alternative power, businesses may want to volunteer the information, in the knowledge that the Revenue can obtain it eventually anyway, and that failure to do so would hold up the enquiry. Many Multi National Enterprises already volunteer the information where they are persuaded that it is relevant.

There are no de minimis limits for an Exchange of Information request. However the Revenue will not generally burden other tax administrations with routine requests where the amount of tax at stake is either small or speculative.

Particular Risk Areas

- Existence of tax haven entities outside the CFC rules that are profitable despite the absence of significant activities carried out in their bases;

- Instances of mismatches between the likely scale of tax haven operations and the level of profits allocated to them; (Although the existence of transactions with affiliates in low tax areas may act as an important indicator, potential transfer pricing issues should not be ignored simply because the other party is in a normal or even high tax rate jurisdiction).

- Profit margins in the UK are lower than in the group generally AND there are reasons to believe that this should not be the case.

- UK company possesses the resources to generate high margin profits yet produces only a routine low margin profit. The Revenue will look for presence of e.g.

- Heavy investment

- highly skilled and remunerated technical or R&D workforce

- intangibles e.g. trade names, know-how, patents etc.

- Royalty or management fee payments that don't appear to make commercial sense AND which substantially impact on UK bottom line e.g.:

  - for a brand name unknown in the UK

  - for technology to which significant value has been added by complex processes carried out in the UK

  - for nebulous bundles of intangibles

- Poor performance over a number of years when there is no obvious prospect of super profits in later years to justify the risk of continuing losses.

- Any period in which changes in intra group contractual arrangements purport to adjust the risk profile, and hence the reward, of the UK group; e.g.:

  - distributor becomes commissionaire (AND net profits fall away)

  - full manufacturer becomes contract manufacturer

  - R&D activities that once generated royalties move to contract basis

  - Cost sharing arrangements introduced

There are no de minimis limits or safe harbours in UK transfer pricing legislation, but regard should be given to both the potential tax at risk and the level of difficulty in establishing the arm's length price.

Where, for example, the cost base is agreed to be £5m, in a case where exceptionally an arm's length cost plus percentage is agreed to be the appropriate method, each 1% increase in the mark up adds only £50,000 to profits. Given the difficulties that can sometimes arise in establishing an arm's length mark up, an enquiry into whether the cost plus percentage should be, for example, 11% rather than 10% may well not be appropriate.

Where on the other hand a company makes an interest free loan of £1m to a well capitalised affiliate, the potential adjustment may still only be in the order of £50-£100,000, but such a case could well merit enquiry because of the relative ease of identifying an arm's length price.

Timetabling

A timetabling framework already exists for transfer pricing cases where applications are accepted for Advance Pricing Agreements (APAs). Further details are set out in Tax Bulletin 43 (page 697) and Statement of Practice 3/99. There, the Inland Revenue aims to complete the APA process in 18 months. An important feature of an APA is that the process is initiated by the company and the timetable does not start until the company has submitted a comprehensive formal proposal. APA formal proposals often contain information that may not be in the power and possession of a UK resident, and hence possibly go beyond the requirements of CTSA. As business operations become more globally integrated a functional analysis of the counterparty to a transaction or details of how the business is structured globally may be relevant in establishing the arms length price. In such circumstances a company may have complied with its obligations under CTSA but still not be in a position to produce readily all the information requested by the Revenue.

A transfer pricing enquiry, unlike an APA, is initiated by the Revenue and the timetable may well need to be longer than 18 months to enable the company to collate the information prepared for CTSA purposes and to obtain any further information requested by the Revenue.

4   Anti-Avoidance

Transfer pricing enquiries can be broken down into four stages

Stage 1	Initial enquiry following risk assessment by the Revenue
Stage 2	Provision by the company of response to Revenue initial enquiries
Stage 3	Revenue's consideration of company's response
Stage 4	Negotiation and agreement

As a result of the risk assessment the Revenue may decide not to make enquiries. Similarly the conclusion of the Revenue's consideration may be that the company's transfer pricing need not be challenged and the enquiry will be closed. A typical analysis of the full enquiry process is illustrated at the end of this article.

Whilst the structure afforded by an APA style timetable can have benefits both for companies and the Revenue, other transfer pricing enquiries may need to be more flexible. In particular, it may not be in the interests of anyone for the timetable for the whole enquiry to be set in stone at the outset. There are advantages in ongoing discussion to agree a timetable for the next stage of the enquiry. So, for example, when the initial enquiry is made there will be an agreement as to how long the company would have to make a response. When the company responds the Revenue will agree with the company a reasonable time for the Revenue response, and so on. Where the agreed timeframe for a particular stage exceeds 3 months it may be appropriate to agree an interim meeting to discuss progress.

Initial Enquiry (following risk assessment)

The initial enquiry should be both focused and comprehensive.

The risk assessment may show that it is not appropriate or feasible to review all cross border transactions in a single enquiry, particularly for large complex groups.

In a pharmaceutical company for example, it may be appropriate to focus on the transfer pricing issues arising from a single drug. In a financial concern it may be appropriate to focus on a single business stream, say fund management, but not capital markets. In an industrial conglomerate there may be little overlap between different businesses so it may be appropriate to deal with them separately.

If there is an existing agreed procedure for reviewing risks with a company this may be particularly helpful in questions of transfer pricing. But once having identified an area of concern, the initial enquiry should be comprehensive, the objective being to procure from the company a justification for its transfer pricing in the relevant area comparable to that of an APA formal proposal. So, for example, where the risk assessment identifies a royalty rate as a concern, the opening enquiry will generally extend to include other cross border transactions such as management fees or purchases of goods.

Requests by the Revenue for information should avoid placing an unnecessary or disproportionate burden upon the company. Sometimes putting the company to considerable trouble is unavoidable but an early meeting to discuss the practicalities of producing and presenting the information could be beneficial. For example:

- A request for information in a particular format that was particularly difficult or incompatible with the way that the company keeps its records could be avoided.

- The Revenue and the company would have an opportunity to ensure that the Revenue's concerns were clear and that the company understood what information was required to address those concerns.

Company's Response to Initial Enquiry

When a company makes a return under CTSA there is a statutory requirement to prepare and retain documentation that demonstrates that its transfer pricing satisfies the arm's length standard. This documentation needs to exist at the time the return is made. This is discussed further in Tax Bulletin 37 published in October 1998.

In response to an initial enquiry, a company will need to make use of the documentation that existed at the time the return was made. Such documentation ought to be capable of being produced quickly. The company might, however, want to provide material going beyond what is contained in the required documentation or going into that material issues in greater detail. Such material might or might not exist at the time the initial enquiry is made. Where it does exist, it can be produced quickly. Where it does not exist, the time necessary to produce it will vary with the nature of the material. Depending on the circumstances and complexity of the issues, it would be reasonable for the company and the Revenue to agree a period of anything up to 6 months to produce the material.

In the event that the company is able to respond within a month, because all the requested documentation exists at the time the return is made, the Revenue does not then have an extra 5 months to complete its own consideration. Nor has the company gained 5 months grace for some later stage in the process. The response times for each stage of the process whatever they are agreed to be- are determined independently of response times in other stages of the process.

Depending on the nature of the transactions under enquiry some of the information re-quested might not be in the power and possession of UK subsidiaries. The Revenue may be able to obtain such information under the Exchange of Information article of the relevant Double Taxation Treaty, but this will inevitably introduce delay. If the process is to be speeded up the company will need to volunteer such information.

Revenue's Consideration of Company's Response

The Revenue will aim to conclude its initial review of the company's position within a timeframe agreed with the company. In the APA model this initial review phase can take up to 6 months, with a further 6 months for obtaining and reviewing additional information. This phase of the transfer pricing enquiry needs to be carefully handled and the time needed will vary greatly from case to case. It is not sensible to be prescriptive but the following is indicative of the steps and timeframes that may be achievable.

- Within 6 months the Revenue aims to conclude its initial review and to share its preliminary conclusions with the company. The Revenue may decide at this stage to close the enquiry. If not the Revenue will say what the concerns are and explain what further information is required and why.

- The company and the Revenue may agree to schedule an interim meeting, for example after 3 months, to discuss the Revenue's preliminary findings and report on progress.

- The Revenue's request for supplementary information will often include arrange-ments for site visits and the opportunity to meet key employees of the company. The purpose of such visits and meetings would be to obtain information required by the Revenue to complete its consideration of the company's position.

- In the next 6 months the company produces the requested information, arranges any site visits and makes further representations in support of the appropriateness of its transfer pricing. Representations and information may be presented at meetings, in writing or through any other convenient and secure media. Again interim meetings to discuss progress can be agreed.

- Following receipt of the supplementary information the Revenue will present its position, either in writing or at a meeting. The enquiry may be closed at this stage. The Revenue may request further information if appropriate (again giving reasons) but ideally the enquiry should be narrowing by now.

6 Banks

In practice there may be more or fewer steps in this phase, and depending on the facts and circumstances of the particular case, one step may take longer than another. The important point is that the Revenue will explain its reasons for any supplementary information requests and for its decision to continue with the enquiry.

Negotiation and settlement

The Revenue and companies have a mutual interest in settling transfer pricing enquiries by negotiation rather than through litigation. The combination of well directed risk assessment and an agreed timetable for enquiries should mean that the negotiating stage is reached after a reasonable period with the disputed areas clearly identified.

Mutual Agreement Procedures

In the event that an adjustment to UK profits results from the enquiry, then the company may be exposed to double taxation. Where Mutual Agreement Procedures are invoked the respective tax administrations will endeavour to eliminate that double taxation. At present the Revenue has an agreed timetable framework for dealing with Mutual Agreement Procedure cases involving the USA and is seeking to extend that framework to other treaty partners. More details about Mutual Agreement Procedures will be published in due course.

Contact names

Richard Gallacher
Tel: 020 7438 6309
Email: Richard.Gallacher@ir.gsi.gov.uk

Hazel Preece
Tel: 020 7438 6823
Email: Hazel.Preece@ir.gsi.gov.uk'

A reference is also added to the article referred to above in relation to accounting periods ending before 1 July 1999 on the application of the transfer pricing rules to employee share scheme costs.

Also, as regards **advance pricing agreements**, it is noted that the address for applications is now Assistant Director (APAs), Revenue Policy, International, Business Tax Group, Victory House, 30-34 Kingsway, London WC2B 6ES (tel. 020-7438 7758; fax 020-7438 6106) or, where oil taxation is involved, Deputy Director (APAs), Revenue Policy, International, Oil Taxation Office (APAs), Melbourne House, Aldwych, London WC2B 4LL (tel. 020-7438 7579; fax 020-7438 6910).

6 Banks

6.2   **Yearly interest.** A reference is added to the case of *Mistletoe Ltd v Flood (Sp C 351)*, *[2003] SSCD 66*, in which a company (M), which had obtained substantial loans from a UK bank (N), became insolvent. N acquired its shares in 1984, and ceased charging interest in 1989. In 1990 N sold its shares in M, and assigned all the interest to a Channel Islands company for nominal consideration. In 1995 M made a payment of interest to the assignee, and failed to deduct tax. The Revenue issued an assessment under *ICTA 1988, Sch 16 para 4(2)* on the basis that M should have deducted tax under *ICTA 1988, s 349(2)*. M appealed, contending that since the debt had been assigned to a Channel Islands company, the effect of *section 349(3)* was that it was not required to deduct tax. The Special Commissioner rejected this contention and dismissed the appeal.

6.8   **Deduction of tax from interest.** It is noted that amendments are made to the regulations by *SI 2002 No 1968*, adding certain dealers in financial instruments to the list of 'deposit-takers' under the scheme.

9   Capital Gains

9.6   **Reconstructions involving transfer of business: anti-avoidance.** It is noted that applications for clearance that the anti-avoidance provisions will not apply should now be addressed to Mohini Sawhney, Fifth Floor, 22 Kingsway, London WC2B 6NR (or, if market-sensitive information is included, to Ray McCann at that address). Applications may be faxed to 020–7438 4409 or e-mailed to reconstructions@gtnet.gov.uk (after advising Ray McCann (on 020–7438 6585) if market-sensitive information is included). Application may now be made in a single letter to the same address for clearance under *TCGA 1992, s 139* and under any one or more of *ICTA 1988, s 215* (demergers, see 29.57 GROUPS OF COMPANIES), *ICTA 1988, s 225* (see 52.6 PURCHASE BY A COMPANY OF ITS OWN SHARES), *ICTA 1988, s 707* (transactions in securities, see Tolley's Income Tax under Anti-Avoidance), *TCGA 1992, s 138(1)* (share exchanges, see Tolley's Capital Gains Tax under Anti-Avoidance), *TCGA 1992, s 140B* (transfer of a UK trade between EC Member States, see 9.8 below), *TCGA 1992, s 140D* (transfer of non-UK trade between EC Member States, see 9.9 below) and *FA 2002, Sch 29 para 88* (see 38.26 INTANGIBLE ASSETS).

Also, as regards the incorporation of Revenue Statement of Practice SP 5/85 within the new statutory definition of 'scheme of reconstruction', the following note is added:

'Under the old definition, *TCGA 1992, s 139* could be used on its own to transfer a business (see the example in the Revenue Capital Gains Manual at CG 52833), but this is no longer possible; under the revised definition, there must be a scheme of reconstruction that meets the conditions of *TCGA 1992, Sch 5AA* and includes an issue of shares under *TCGA 1992, s 136*.'

References are also added to the Revenue Capital Gains Manual, CG 52707b, CG 52709, CG 52720–52733 for various definitions and examples.

9.8   **Transfer of UK trade between companies in different EC Member States.** The paragraph after list (*a*), (*b*), concerning clearance in relation to (*b*), is revised as follows.

'Advance clearance in relation to (*b*) above may be obtained from the Board on the application of the companies, subject to the same conditions and appeal procedures as apply to clearances under *TCGA 1992, s 138* (see Tolley's Capital Gains Tax under Anti-Avoidance). Applications for clearance should be addressed to Mohini Sawhney, Fifth Floor, 22 Kingsway, London WC2B 6NR (or, if market-sensitive information is included, to Ray McCann at that address). Applications may be faxed to 020–7438 4409 or e-mailed to reconstructions@gtnet.gov.uk (after advising Ray McCann (on 020–7438 6585) if market-sensitive information is included). Application may be made in a single letter to the same address for clearance under *TCGA 1992, s 140B* and under any one or more of *ICTA 1988, s 215* (demergers, see 29.57 GROUPS OF COMPANIES), *ICTA 1988, s 225* (see 52.6 PURCHASE BY A COMPANY OF ITS OWN SHARES), *ICTA 1988, s 707* (transactions in securities, see Tolley's Income Tax under Anti-Avoidance), *TCGA 1992, s 138(1)* (share exchanges, see Tolley's Capital Gains Tax under Anti-Avoidance), *TCGA 1992, s 139(5)* (reconstructions involving the transfer of a business, see 9.6 above), *TCGA 1992, s 140D* (transfer of non-UK trade between EC Member States, see 9.9 below) and *FA 2002, Sch 29 para 88* (see 38.26 INTANGIBLE ASSETS).'

9.9   **Transfer of non-UK trade between companies in different EC Member States.** The paragraph concerning clearance in relation to sub-paragraph (*e*) is revised as follows.

'Advance clearance in relation to (*e*) above may be obtained from the Board on the application of the UK company, subject to the same conditions and appeal procedures as apply to clearances under *TCGA 1992, s 138* (see Tolley's Capital Gains Tax under Anti-Avoidance). Applications for clearance should be addressed to Mohini Sawhney, Fifth Floor, 22 Kingsway, London WC2B 6NR (or, if market-sensitive information is included, to Ray McCann at that address). Applications may be faxed to 020–7438 4409 or e-mailed to reconstructions@gtnet.gov.uk (after advising Ray McCann (on 020–7438 6585) if market-sensitive information is included). Application may be made in a single letter to the same address for clearance under *TCGA 1992, s 140D* and under any one or more of *ICTA 1988, s 215* (demergers, see 29.57 GROUPS OF COMPANIES), *ICTA 1988, s 225* (see 52.6 PURCHASE BY A COMPANY OF ITS OWN SHARES), *ICTA 1988, s 707* (transactions in securities, see Tolley's Income Tax under Anti-Avoidance), *TCGA 1992, s 138(1)* (share exchanges, see Tolley's Capital Gains Tax under Anti-Avoidance), *TCGA 1992, s 139(5)* (reconstructions involving the transfer of a business, see 9.6 above), *TCGA 1992, s 140B* (transfer of a UK trade between EC Member States, see 9.9 below) and *FA 2002, Sch 29 para 88* (see 38.26 INTANGIBLE ASSETS).'

9.54   **Depreciatory transactions.** It is noted that the Special Commissioners' decision in *Whitehall Electric Investments Ltd* is now reported at *[2002] SSCD 229*.

10   Capital Gains — Substantial Shareholdings

10.1   **Introduction.** A general reference is added to the Revenue Capital Gains Manual, CG 53000–53240.

10.4   **Exemption for shares.** The following paragraph is added.

'The exemption is available even where the shares disposed of are not the shares that meet the substantial shareholding requirement at (*a*) above. If (*a*) above is met in relation to ordinary shares (and (*b*) and (*c*) are also met), a disposal of a holding of, say, fixed-rate preference shares in the investee company will qualify for the exemption, irrespective of the size and duration of that holding. (Revenue Capital Gains Manual, CG 53155).'

10.5   **Exemption for assets related to shares.** The following paragraphs are added.

'As regards (2) above, a convertible or exchangeable security is not an asset related to shares if, when the conversion etc. rights were granted, there was no more than a negligible likelihood that they would be exercised to any significant extent. It is therefore not possible to bring a security within the scope of the exemption by attaching some spurious or extremely remote rights to convertibility in the event of some unlikely occurrence. (Revenue Capital Gains Manual, CG 53010).'

Certain securities, options etc. are outside the scope of corporation tax on chargeable gains, and thus outside the exemptions in this chapter, due to their falling within the special LOAN RELATIONSHIPS (44) or FINANCIAL INSTRUMENTS AND DERIVATIVE CONTRACTS (25) rules. (Revenue Capital Gains Manual, CG 53010).'

10.7   **Anti-avoidance.** A new final paragraph is added as follows.

'The Revenue expect cases where this anti-avoidance rule is in point to be unusual and infrequent. It is a question of fact as to whether a gain wholly (or wholly but for an insubstantial part — interpreted by the Revenue as 20% or less) represents untaxed profits; this involves looking at how the consideration obtained for the disposal by Company A is derived from assets held directly or indirectly by Company B. Profits are not 'untaxed' if they are simply covered by a specific relief or if they represent dividends which are themselves paid out of taxed profits. If a gain represents both taxed and untaxed profits, it should be taken as first representing taxed profits, with only any remaining balance representing untaxed profits. (Revenue Statement of Practice SP 5/02, 29 October 2002). The Revenue have also published on their website some practical illustrations of when the anti-avoidance rule will or may apply and when it will not.'

The full text of the Statement of Practice is as follows.

'SP5/2002: Exemptions for companies' gains on substantial shareholdings – sole or main benefit test – Paragraph 5 Schedule 7AC Taxation of Chargeable Gains Act 1992.

Introduction

1. The regime in Schedule 7AC TCGA 1992 ("Schedule 7AC") for the exemption of gains on disposals of substantial shareholdings will apply to disposals of shares (or an interest in, or an asset related to, shares) by companies which have held a substantial shareholding for at least 12 months where -

- the company holding the shares (or an interest in, or an asset related to shares) is a trading company or a member of a trading group, and

- the shares in question are shares in a trading company or the holding company of a trading group or subgroup.

2. The exemptions provided by the regime may create opportunities for manipulation. The provisions therefore contain an anti-avoidance rule at paragraph 5 of Schedule 7AC. This is aimed at tax-driven arrangements which are intended to exploit any of the exemptions.

3. We expect cases where the anti-avoidance rule is in point to be unusual and infrequent.

4. In what follows, references to paragraphs are to paragraphs of Schedule 7AC.

Outline of the anti-avoidance rule

5. Paragraph 5 is aimed at "arrangements" from which the "sole or main benefit" that can be expected to be derived is that a gain on a disposal will be exempt by virtue of an exemption in Part 1 of Schedule 7AC. The remedy is to deny exemption on any gain arising on the relevant disposal. "Arrangements" is defined widely and includes "any scheme, agreement or understanding, whether or not legally enforceable".

6. Paragraph 5(1) provides that certain events must occur in pursuance of the arrangements before the "sole or main benefit test" in paragraph 5(2) can apply:

- an untaxed gain must accrue to a company ("company A") on a disposal of shares, or an interest in shares or an asset related to shares, in another company ("company B"),

- and before the gain accrued either

- company A acquired control of company B, or the same person or persons acquired control of both companies, or

- there was a significant change of trading activities affecting company B at a time when it was controlled by company A, or when both companies were controlled by the same person or persons.

7. Paragraph 5(5) provides that there is a "significant change of trading activities affecting company B" if -

- there is a major change in the nature or conduct of a trade carried on by company B or a 51% subsidiary of company B, or

- there is a major change in the scale of the activities of a trade carried on by company B or a 51% subsidiary of company B, or

- company B or a subsidiary of company B begins to carry on a trade.

8. A "major change in the nature or conduct of the trade" in this legislation has the same meaning as in S768 ICTA 1988.

9. For the purposes of paragraph 5(1) a gain is "untaxed" if the gain, or all of it but a part that is not substantial, represents profits that have not been brought into account (in the United Kingdom or elsewhere) for the purposes of tax on profits for a period ending on or before the date of the disposal. "Profits" for these purposes means income or gains, including unrealised income or gains. But profits are not "untaxed profits" if an amount in respect of these profits is apportioned to and chargeable on a UK-resident company under the controlled foreign company rules for an accounting period of the company ending on or before the date of the disposal.

Application of the rule

10. It will be a question of fact in any particular case as to whether a gain wholly, or wholly except for a part which is not substantial, represents untaxed profits. Broadly, this will involve looking at how the consideration obtained for the shares is derived from assets held directly or indirectly by company B.

11. It will usually be obvious when profits are "untaxed" within the meaning of paragraph 5. For example, unrealised profits on capital assets will be untaxed profits. It is impossible to provide a comprehensive catalogue of all situations where the gain will represent untaxed profits but some examples of situations where the profits will not be untaxed profits for the purpose of paragraph 5 would be -

- a dividend received by a holding company that is paid out of taxed profits of the subsidiary;

- where the profits in question themselves represent an exempt gain on disposal of a substantial shareholding;

- where no tax is payable on profits because they are covered by a specific relief (e.g. loss relief).

12. In many cases a gain will represent both taxed and untaxed profits. In these circumstances, the gain should be taken as first representing the taxed profits and only any balance which then remains as representing untaxed profits.

13. In the context of this legislation we interpret "substantial" as meaning more than 20%.

14. Even if on this basis the gain wholly, or wholly except for a part which is not substantial, represents untaxed profits, the exemption would be denied only if -

- each of the circumstances set out in paragraph 5(1) occurs in pursuance of arrangements, and

- the sole or main benefit that could be expected to arise from the arrangements is that the gain accruing on the disposal would otherwise be exempt under Schedule 7AC, and

- from the outset the sole or main benefit expected to arise from the arrangements is the achievement of that outcome.'

10.9   **Holding period.** The following note is added in the first paragraph.

'Shares are treated as having been held for such a period if, for example, they were acquired at any time on 15 June 2002 and sold at any time on 14 June 2003; they do not have to be held on the anniversary of the acquisition. (Revenue Capital Gains Manual, CG 53008).'

10.11   **Trading company.** It is noted that a Revenue Tax Bulletin article (December 2002 pp 982–987), reproduced below, confirms that 'substantial' in connection with the extent of a company's activities is taken to mean 'more than 20%', and that 'activities' in this context is interpreted by the Revenue to mean 'what a company does', so that the expression in itself includes engaging in trading activities, making and holding investments, planning, holding meetings and so on.

It is also noted that many of the expressions used in this section are considered further in the same article. A company may ask its tax district to give a view on its status for these purposes, but any opinion expressed will be subject to revision to the extent that it relates to a time for which the full facts are not yet available. The article lists the information the inspector will require to enable him to form a view.

The full text of the article is as follows.

'TAXATION OF CHARGEABLE GAINS — TAPER RELIEF AND EXEMPTION FOR DISPOSALS BY COMPANIES WITH SUBSTANTIAL SHAREHOLDINGS: MEANING OF "TRADING COMPANY", "TRADING GROUP", "TRADING SUB-GROUP", "HOLDING GROUP" AND RELATED ISSUES — PARAGRAPHS 22(1), 22A AND 22B OF SCHEDULE A1, AND PARAGRAPHS 20, 21, 22 AND 26 OF SCHEDULE 7AC, TO THE TAXATION OF CHARGEABLE GAINS ACT 1992

We have been asked to offer guidance on the meaning of certain statutory terms for the purposes of Capital Gains Tax taper relief and the new exemption for disposals by companies with substantial shareholdings. This article provides that guidance. The relevant legislation was enacted by Finance Act 2002. Words in italics in this article denote expressions that are defined in the legislation.

Introduction

Tax Bulletin 53 (June 2001) [TB53] included an article which explained the Inland Revenue's approach to interpreting the meaning of *trading company* and *holding company* of a *trading group* for the purposes of taper relief. Paragraphs 9 and 10 of Schedule 10 to Finance Act 2002 have revised the definitions of *trading company* and *trading group* for taper relief purposes for periods of ownership from 17 April 2002. There is also a new definition of *holding company* (see paragraph 4 of Schedule 10). Further, the qualifications for investment in a *joint venture company* as they affect the question as to whether a company or group was a *trading company* or *trading group* during a period have been relaxed (see paragraphs 11 and 12 of Schedule 10). The definitions described in TB 53 therefore now apply only for periods of ownership before 17 April 2002 even where the disposal takes place on or after that date.

Finance Act 2002 also introduced Schedule 7AC into the Taxation of Chargeable Gains Act [TCGA] 1992. This brings in an exemption regime for disposals by companies with substantial shareholdings [SSE]. The SSE legislation employs some of the same concepts as taper relief (e.g. *trading company*, *trading group*). Other definitions (e.g. *trading subgroup*) are relevant only to SSE.

This article considers further the meanings of these and other expressions in the light of the legislation introduced by Finance Act 2002 and, in particular, confirms that:

- Although the definition of company for taper relief is not identical to that used for SSE and the definition of a *group of companies* for taper relief is different from that of a *group* for SSE, the definitions of *trading company* and *trading group* are essentially common to both regimes.

- For taper relief, the changes to the wording of the definitions of *trading company* and *trading group* align the statute with existing practice. They are not intended to alter the substance of the original definitions, or to have different meanings before and on or after 17 April 2002.

Subject to the different meanings of *company* and *group* in the two regimes, the explanations in this article apply equally to both reliefs. They draw on the existing guidance in TB53, which continues to apply for taper relief in respect of periods of ownership before 17 April 2002. Because the essentials of the definitions of *trading company* and *trading group* for taper relief remain the same, much of what was said in TB53 is repeated here although the text has been updated to reflect the new wording of the legislation.

The legislation

Taper Relief: Shares as business assets and qualifying companies

Paragraph 4 of Schedule A1 TCGA 1992 sets out the conditions for shares to qualify as business assets and paragraph 6 of Schedule A1 (as amended by section 67 Finance Act 2000) sets out the rules for a company to be a *qualifying company* in relation to a person making a disposal of shares in a company. Where a company is a *qualifying company* in relation to that person the business assets rate of taper relief may be due wholly or in part on any chargeable gain arising on the disposal. The question as to whether a company is a *qualifying company* may also be relevant to persons who dispose of assets used for a trade carried on by a company.

Substantial shareholdings

The SSE legislation provides that from 1 April 2002 disposals of shares (or *interests in shares* or *assets related to shares* — as defined in paragraphs 29 and 30 of Schedule 7AC TCGA 1992) by companies with substantial shareholdings do not result in chargeable gains, or allowable losses, provided certain conditions are met. Two of these conditions are that, at certain times determined by reference to the date of the disposal in question

- the company making the disposal is a member of a trading group or, if not a member of a *group*, is a *trading company*;

- the shares are in a company that is itself a *trading company*, or the *holding company* of either a *trading group* or a *trading subgroup*.

Definitions and interpretations

Trading company

A *trading company* is "… a company carrying on trading activities whose activities do not include to a substantial extent activities other than trading activities" (paragraph 22A(1) of Schedule A1 TCGA 1992 and paragraph 20(1) of Schedule 7AC TCGA 1992).

Holding company, group and subgroup

For taper relief, paragraph 22(1) of Schedule A1 TCGA 1992 defines a *group of companies* as "… a company which has one or more *51% subsidiaries*, together with those subsidiaries". For periods of ownership from 17 April 2002, paragraph 22(1) of Schedule A1 defines a *holding company* as "… a company that has one or more *51% subsidiaries*". The previous definition, which applies for such periods prior to that date, makes it necessary to determine the extent of a company's business (excluding its own trade, if any) which consists of holding shares in its *51% subsidiaries*. A company is a *holding company* at any time prior to 17 April 2002 when its business consists wholly or mainly of holding shares in its *51% subsidiaries*. This test does not apply for periods of ownership from 17 April 2002. From that date, a company is a "*holding company*" at any time when it has a *51% subsidiary*.

In the SSE regime a *holding company* is defined differently to encompass *subgroups* as well as *groups*. But *holding companies* are defined in essentially the same way for both taper and SSE purposes. Paragraph 26 of Schedule 7AC defines a *group* and membership of a group by reference to the normal capital gains group rules in section 170 TCGA 1992 except that references in section 170 to 75% subsidiaries are replaced by references to *51% subsidiaries*. Paragraph 26 defines a *subgroup* as a collection of companies that would themselves form an SSE group but for the fact that one of them is a *51% subsidiary* of another company. A *holding company* is then defined

- for an SSE *group*, as the company described in section 170 TCGA 1992 as the principal company of the group, and

- for a *subgroup*, as the company that would be the *holding company* of an SSE *group* but for the fact that it is a *51% subsidiary* of another company.

The taper relief and SSE legislation define a *51% subsidiary* by reference to the meaning given by section 838 of the Income and Corporation Taxes Act (ICTA) 1988 (see paragraph 22(1) of Schedule A1 TCGA 1992 for taper relief and paragraph 26(4) of Schedule 7AC TCGA 1992 for SSE). A company is a *51% subsidiary* of another company for taper relief and SSE purposes if the second company owns directly or indirectly more than 50% of the *ordinary share capital* of the first company.

Ordinary share capital is defined for the purposes of the Tax Acts (which includes the provisions relating to corporation tax) in section 832(1) ICTA 1988 (this is applied for the purposes of Schedule A1 TCGA 1992 by paragraph 22(1) of that Schedule). The meaning is extended for the purposes of the definition of *51% subsidiary* which applies for SSE purposes (but not for taper relief purposes) to include any share capital of a registered industrial and provident society (see paragraph 26(4) of Schedule 7AC TCGA 1992). Some companies do not have ordinary share capital (e.g. some Limited Liability Companies in the United States, see Tax Bulletin 51). Such companies cannot therefore be *51% subsidiaries* of other companies.

Trading group and trading subgroup

Paragraph 22B(1) of Schedule A1 TCGA 1992, for taper relief, and paragraph 21 of Schedule 7AC TCGA 1992, for SSE, define what is a *trading group* in the same terms. The definition parallels that of a *trading company* so that a *trading group* is a group one or more of whose members carries on *trading activities* provided the activities of the group as a whole do not include, to a substantial extent, activities other than *trading activities*. The activities of the members of a group are treated as one business. Intra-group activities are disregarded for the purpose of determining whether the group is a *trading group*. So, for example, where one group company lets a property to another group company, the letting activity would be disregarded for this purpose. However, this netting off approach does not extend to transactions with joint venture companies that are not members of the group. So, letting property to such a joint venture company would count as an activity of the lessor.

In identifying companies whose shares might qualify for SSE exemption the concept of a *trading subgroup* is used to describe part of a group. It is defined in paragraph 22 of Schedule 7AC in the same way as a *trading group*, but with references to *trading group* changed to *trading subgroup* where appropriate. Intra-subgroup activities are disregarded in the same way as intra-group activities when determining whether a subgroup is a *trading subgroup*. However, intra-group activities between a member of the subgroup and another group company that is not in the subgroup are not disregarded in considering the status of the subgroup.

Trading activities

Paragraphs 22A and 22B of Schedule A1 TCGA 1992 and paragraphs 20, 21 and 22 of Schedule 7AC TCGA 1992 define *trading activities*. For a *company/group/subgroup* these are activities carried on by the *company/a member of the group/subgroup*

(a)   in the course of, or for the purposes of, a trade being carried on by it/any member of the group/subgroup,

(b)   for the purposes of a trade that it/any member of the group/subgroup is preparing to carry on,

(c)   with a view to its/any member of the group/subgroup acquiring or starting to carry on a trade, or

(d)   with a view to its/any member of the group/subgroup acquiring a *significant interest* in the share capital of another company that -

    (i)   is a *trading company* or the *holding company of a trading group* (or a trading subgroup in SSE), and

    (ii)   if the acquiring company is a member of a group, is not a member of that group.

However, activities within (c) and (d) count as trading activities only if the company/group member/subgroup member starts to carry on the trade, or acquires the shares, as soon as is reasonably practicable in the circumstances. For the purposes of (d) a *significant interest* is such an interest as

• would make the company acquired a member of the same group/subgroup as the acquiring company, or

• would result in the acquiring company having a *qualifying shareholding* in a *joint venture company* without making the two companies members of the same group (see paragraph 23 of Schedule A1 for taper relief and paragraph 24 of Schedule 7AC for SSE for definitions of *qualifying shareholding* and *joint venture company*).

The word "activities" is not defined in the statute but in this context we interpret it to mean what a company does. Activities will therefore include engaging in trading operations, making and holding investments, planning, holding meetings and so forth. The legislation makes explicit that a company may have trading activities both when it is trading and before it commences to trade.

Trade

The following are trades for the purposes of taper relief and SSE:

• anything that is a trade, profession or vocation within the meaning of the Income Tax Acts and is conducted on a commercial basis with a view to the realisation of profits (paragraph 22(1) of Schedule A1 TCGA 1992 and paragraph 27 of Schedule 7AC TCGA 1992), and

• any Schedule A business (within the meaning of ICTA 1988) which consists in the commercial letting of holiday accommodation in the United Kingdom (section 241(3) TCGA 1992 as amended by paragraph 3 of Schedule 8 to Finance Act 2002).

We confirm that activities, such as farming, that are treated as a trade by section 53 ICTA 1988, are trades for the purposes of the Income Tax Acts.

In the course of, or for the purposes of, a trade

We accept that an activity is carried on in the course of, or for the purposes of, a trade if it is carried on in the process of conducting or preparing to carry on the trade. So, for example, where a company renegotiates an ongoing trading contract relating to its trade this will be an activity undertaken "in the course of" its trade. It will be clear in most cases whether an activity that a company undertakes is carried on in the course of, or for the purposes of, its trade or not. But similar transactions can be undertaken for different reasons depending on the facts.

For instance, a company may buy some land. If the company is a property developer and buys the land as trading stock, or a manufacturer and buys it to provide a site for a factory it intends to build to house its manufacturing process, the buying of the land would probably count as a trading activity. However, if a company buys the land so as to earn future rental income, or for potential capital growth, the buying of the land would not normally be a trading activity.

Normally, making an investment that yields investment income would not count as a trading activity. However, there are a number of circumstances where such activities could be undertaken in the course of, or for the purposes of, a company's trade.

An investment may be so closely related to the conduct of a trade that it effectively forms an integral part of the trade. For example, a travel agent may be required to keep a fixed level of cash on deposit for bonding requirements. Or a company might receive a large payment, perhaps from selling a shareholding or on the completion of a major contract, and earmark the funds for some particular trade purposes, such as to meet some demonstrable trading liability or expand the trade in the near future. The short-term lodgement of such surplus funds, for example in an interest-bearing deposit account or in bonds or equities, could count as a trading activity. Alternatively, the company may intend distributing the monies received to its members. Depending on the facts, temporarily investing such funds until they can be distributed could count as being an activity undertaken for the purposes of the company's trade, since paying out the profits generated by a trade can count as a trading activity. This would be the case, for example, where the payment of an annual dividend depended on a meeting of the company's shareholders. Whether or not making and holding investments are part of a company's trading activities is a question of fact that can be determined only by reference to all the relevant circumstances.

Preparing to carry on a trade

The legislation specifically provides that trading activities include activities for the purposes of a trade that a company is preparing to carry on. This encompasses the situation where a particular trade is about to be started but the company has to carry out certain activities first. It also covers cases where an existing trade, which is currently being carried on by another person, will be acquired. The trading activities here may include one or more of: developing a business plan for carrying on the trade, acquiring premises, hiring staff, ordering materials and incurring pre-trading expenditure for the purposes of the trade to be carried on.

Acquiring or starting to carry on a trade, or acquiring shares in a _trading company_

Activities that a company undertakes with a view to acquiring or starting to carry on a trade, or acquiring a significant interest in the share capital of a _trading company_, may count as trading activities.

It is quite common for a company to dispose of its trade (or main trading subsidiary) and to invest (or put on deposit) the cash proceeds while it looks around to acquire a new trade or trading subsidiary. A company, group or subgroup temporarily in this position and actively seeking to acquire a new trade or trading subsidiary might still be a _trading company_, trading _group_ or _trading subgroup_ if it does not have substantial non-trading activities.

Trading activities here include assessing the potential viability of a trade which the company, group or subgroup is considering carrying on and other such activities even though they are not directly preparatory to the carrying on of the particular trade under consideration. So, a company, group or subgroup which has surplus cash that it intends to use to acquire a trade, or to start up one from scratch, which is actively evaluating a number of possible trades may be engaged in trading activities. However, such activities are trading activities only if an acquisition is made, or a new trade is commenced, as soon as is reasonably practicable in the circumstances.

As soon as is reasonably practicable in the circumstances

Rather than impose a fixed time limit, the legislation allows companies whatever time is reasonable, having regard to the particular circumstances, to prepare to carry on a new trade or to acquire a trade or *trading company*. What is reasonably practicable in the circumstances will depend on the facts in each case. For example, a company may be in negotiations to acquire a *trading company* but owing to circumstances beyond its control the purchase is delayed. There might be, for example, a problem with the vendor proving title to the company's assets. In such a case we would not suggest that the acquisition had not been made as soon as was reasonably practicable in the circumstances where this was the reason for the delay.

Substantial

Most companies groups and subgroups will have some activities that are not *trading activities*. The legislation provides that such companies and groups still count as trading if their activities "… do not include to a *substantial extent* activities other than trading activities". The phrase *substantial extent* is used in various parts of the TCGA 1992 to provide some flexibility in interpreting a provision without opening the door to widespread abuse. We consider that substantial in this context means more than 20%. The numerical tests in the SSE legislation for a shareholding to be a substantial shareholding refer to 10% or more, but this use of the word substantial is specifically applied only for the purpose of deciding whether a company holds a substantial shareholding in another company (paragraph 8(1) of Schedule 7AC TCGA 1992).

How should a company's non-trading activities be measured to assess whether they are substantial? Some or all of the following are among the measures that might be taken into account in reviewing a particular company's status.

Income from non-trading activities

For example, a company may have a trade but also let an investment property. If the company's receipts from the letting are substantial in comparison to its combined trading and letting receipts then, on this measure in isolation, the company would probably not be a *trading company*.

The asset base of the company

If the value of a company's non-trading assets is substantial in comparison with its total assets then again, on this measure, this could point towards it not being a *trading company*. If a company retains an asset it previously used, but no longer uses, for the purposes of its trade, this may not be a trading activity (but see below regarding surplus trading premises). In some cases it might be appropriate to take account of intangible assets (e.g. goodwill) that are not shown on a balance sheet in considering a company's assets. Current market value and amounts given by way of consideration for assets may both be appropriate measures of the relative extents of a company's trading and other activities. Which measure is appropriate will depend on the facts in each case.

Expenses incurred, or time spent, by officers and employees of the company in undertaking its activities

For example, if a substantial proportion of the expenses of a company were to be incurred on non-trading activities then, on this measure, the company would not be a *trading company*.

Or a company may devote a substantial amount of its staff resources, by time or costs incurred, to non-trading activities.

The company's history may be relevant. For example, at a particular instant certain receipts may be substantial compared to total receipts but, if looked at on a longer timescale, they may not be substantial compared to other receipts over that longer period. Looked at in this context, therefore, a company might be able to show that it was a *trading company* over a period, even where that period may have included particular points in time when, for example, non-trade receipts amounted to a substantial proportion of total receipts.

It may be that some indicators point in one direction and others the opposite way. We would weigh up the impact of each of the measures in the context of an individual case. If the Inspector was unable to agree the status of a particular company for a period then the issue could be established only as a question of fact before the Commissioners. However, we anticipate that such cases will be relatively rare.

Surplus trading property

We have been asked how property owned by a company and surplus to its immediate business requirements should be dealt with. Each case would need to be considered in light of the facts. We would not, for example, regard the following as necessarily indicating a non-trading activity:

- letting part of the trading premises;

- letting properties that are no longer required for the purpose of the trade in question, where the company's objective is to sell those properties;

- subletting property where it would be impractical or uneconomic in terms of the trade to assign or surrender the lease. For example, the benefit derived from disposing of the lease may be outweighed by the reverse premium payable;

- the acquisition of property (whether vacant or already let) where it can be shown that the intention is that it will be brought into use for trading activities.

Investments in joint venture companies

Where a company has a *qualifying shareholding* in a *joint venture company* (as defined in paragraph 23 of Schedule A1 TCGA 1992 for taper relief and in paragraph 24 of Schedule 7AC TCGA 1992 for SSE) then, provided the *joint venture company* is not in the *same group* as the company,

- the holding of any shares or securities that the company holds in the *joint venture company* is disregarded, and

- the company is treated as carrying on a proportion of the activities of the *joint venture company* equal to the proportion of that company's ordinary share capital it holds

in determining whether: (a) the company is a *trading company*, (b) a group that the company is a member of is a *trading group*, and (c) the company is the *holding company* of a *trading group* or *trading subgroup*.

Shares and other assets held otherwise than as investments

Companies may acquire shares or other assets for reasons other than investment. For example, companies may be paid in shares instead of cash as fees for services rendered or work carried out. Once such shares have been acquired the reasons for retaining them will need to be considered in order to determine whether or not their retention means that a company has non-trading activities. Among other issues, we should need to know the reasons why the shares were taken in settling a trade debt and whether they can reasonably be turned into cash or otherwise exchanged to meet trading requirements.

A company may have to hold shares in another company as a pre-requisite to trading (for example, companies may be expected to own shares in a trade organisation). In such cases we should want to know the reasons for holding such a share in order to determine whether the holding was a trading activity.

Corporate Venturing Scheme [CVS]

Investments in shares made under the CVS are investments like any others and the holding of such shares is unlikely to count as a trading activity in its own right. However, the CVS works in such a way that a company that qualifies for CVS investment relief is unlikely to have more than the 20% non-trading activity that would stop it being a *trading company* for taper relief and SSE purposes.

What to do if you want to know if a company is a trading company or the holding company of a trading group or subgroup

If you want to establish whether a company in which you held shares was a *qualifying company* for taper relief purposes while you owned the shares, our advice is that, in the first instance, you should seek advice from the company. The company will usually be able to tell you if its activities were such that it was a *trading company* (or the *holding company* of a *trading group*) so that it could have been a *qualifying company* so far as you were concerned.

Similarly, if a corporate shareholder planning to sell shares in a company wants some indication of whether that company is a *trading company* (or the *holding company* of a *trading group* or *trading subgroup*) for SSE purposes, it should ask the company concerned.

In either case, the responsibility for ascertaining the status of a company referred to in your tax return rests with you and you will need to take a view and make your return on this basis: you may wish, where applicable, to point out in the return that you made an unsuccessful approach to the company for confirmation of its status. Alternatively, the Inspector dealing with your returns may be able to provide a post-transaction ruling under the Code of Practice 10 procedures. For reasons of confidentiality the Inspector dealing with the company's tax affairs will not be able to correspond with you regarding its status.

A company may wish to establish its status for various reasons:

- so that it can tell its non-corporate shareholders when it has been a *trading company* (or the *holding company* of a *trading group*) for taper relief purposes;

- when it is planning to sell shares, the gain on the disposal may be exempted by the SSE legislation and it wants to know if it may qualify as a sole *trading company* (or a member of a *trading group*) for SSE purposes during the period specified in paragraph 18(1) of Schedule 7AC TCGA 1992;

- when its corporate shareholders are planning to sell shares in the company and the gain on the disposal may be exempted by the SSE legislation, the shareholders may want to know if the company may qualify as a *trading company* (or the *holding company* of a *trading group* or *trading subgroup*) for SSE purpose during the period specified in paragraph 19(1) of Schedule 7AC.

In these circumstances Inspectors will, where there is uncertainty as to the company's status, respond to requests for their view in accordance with Code of Practice 10 and this article.

Any opinion that a company is or is not a *trading company*, a group is a *trading group* or a subgroup is a *trading subgroup* can relate only to the period under consideration. It is possible for a company, group or subgroup to change its status at any time, as its business or activities change.

Inspectors will usually be able to give a firm opinion on the status of a company for periods that have ended where all the relevant facts have been provided. Any view expressed which relates to a time for which facts are not yet available will be subject to revision. Future events may put a different perspective on the true nature of the activities of a company, group or subgroup during a previous period.

Because of the inherent difficulty in giving a view based on uncertain information, in some cases those involved may prefer to wait until all the relevant facts are known before approaching the Inspector.

So that the company's Inspector can form a view, the company should set out for its Inspector:

- the reason why it is seeking the Inspector's opinion and the period over which the company wants the Inspector to consider its status;

- all the facts that the company considers relevant in measuring the extent of its trading and its non trading activities and, where appropriate, the assumptions it has made in describing what it expects its activities to comprise over the part of the period falling after the latest point for which data is available;

- why the company considers that there is uncertainty as to its status;

- the company's conclusion as to its status, and why it considers, if applicable, that the measures that point in that direction outweigh those pointing in the opposite direction; and

- (for SSE purposes) what disposal is being contemplated and when it is expected that the transaction will be completed.

The Inspector will offer his or her opinion whenever this is practicable and, if this differs from the company's view, explain the reasons for that difference.'

11   Charities

11.10   **Gift Aid donations by companies: donations made on or after 1 April 2000.** The following paragraph is added:

'Acknowledgement of a donor in the charity's literature does not amount to a benefit *provided that* it does not take the form of an advertisement for the donor's business (see para 3.27 of the Revenue guide referred to below).'

and the following note is appended:

'See generally the Revenue website at www.inlandrevenue.gov.uk/charities/chapter_3.htm for a detailed guide to Gift Aid.'

11.15   **Gifts of medical supplies and equipment.** The following paragraph is added.

'No claim form or entry on the CT600 tax return is required for operation of the relief. For this and for the "humanitarian purposes" requirement, and the broad scope of "medical supplies or equipment", see the article on the operation of the scheme in the Revenue Tax Bulletin October 2002, pp 975–977.'

The Revenue Tax Bulletin article referred to is reproduced below.

'SECTION 55 FA 2002: TAX RELIEF FOR GIFTS OF MEDICAL SUPPLIES AND EQUIPMENT

Companies in the pharmaceutical industry sometimes donate medical products to countries in the developing world. This may be done in response to emergency appeals, but is more commonly done as part of a structured, long-term programme, aimed at controlling a disease endemic in a poor country.

Up to now the difficulty has been that UK companies which took part in such programmes and which gave products direct, rather than through a charity, risked being taxed on those gifts. This is because of the case law established in Sharkey v Wernher (36TC275) concerning goods taken out of the business other than by way of a sale in the normal course of trade. This requires that an amount equal to the market value of the product donated be added back to the company's taxable profits to represent the sales foregone.

The Government has addressed this in Section 55 of the Finance Act 2002. The section provides that no such tax charge will arise where companies make gifts of medical supplies and equipment out of trading stock, provided that these are made for humanitarian purposes and for human use. It also ensures that the costs of transportation, distribution and delivery are tax deductible. The measure builds on Section 83A ICTA 1988, which was introduced by the Finance Act 1999. Section 83A provides a similar relief for donations of trading stock (of any kind) made to charitable bodies in the UK.

We have been asked whether this measure will encourage inappropriate donations. We do not think so given that companies already receive relief for donations in kind made to UK charities and there is no evidence to suggest that this has led to abuse. The instances that have been drawn to our attention appear to arise in countries whose tax regimes provide an extra credit for stock donations. Our legislation only removes a tax charge, and leaves the donor company in much the same financial position as if it had scrapped the stock.

The World Health Organisation has drawn up guidelines on responsible donations of medicines, covering matters such as their suitability, shelf life, labelling, and delivery. These can be accessed at www.who.int/medicines/library/par/who-edm-par-99-4/who-edm-par-99-4.doc. We will accept that donations which meet the WHO guidelines will also satisfy our condition of being made for humanitarian purposes.

No claim form is being provided, and there is no obligation to make entries in the tax return or computations referring to this relief. Any company which requires further information about Section 55 may consult the Inspector who handles its day to day tax affairs.

Guidance on Section 55 FA 2002 will be included in the Inspectors Manual. An advance copy of this material is set out below.

IM 1142a : introduction

S55 Finance Act 2002

FA02/S55 provides a relief supplemental to ICTA88/S83A for corporate donations of medical supplies and medical equipment for humanitarian purposes anywhere in the world, without restriction to registered charities.

IM1142b : background

Pharmaceutical companies sometimes take part in programmes aimed at the treatment or eradication of diseases in developing countries by supplying medicines or vaccines, or equipment, free of charge. They do this in co-operation with the public health authorities in the recipient country, and often under the auspices of international aid organisations or the World Heath Organisation. In addition, companies may make occasional donations in response to an emergency appeal from a country affected by natural disaster.

IM1142c : open market value rule disapplied

Where a company makes a gift, out of trading stock, of medical supplies or medical equipment, for human use, and for humanitarian purposes, then the case law rule requiring the open market value of the gift to be brought in as a trading receipt is dis-applied. In addition, any costs incurred in the transport and distribution of the donated products will be deductible in the Case I computation.

IM1142d : benefit received by the donor or a connected person

Exceptionally, if the company or any connected person receives a benefit from the making of the gift, the amount of the benefit is to be brought into charge as a taxable profit. An example would be if a UK manufacturer donated products on the understanding that an overseas affiliate was given preferential terms for the supply of other goods or services.

IM1142e : de-regulatory nature of legislation

This is intended as a de-regulatory measure. No claim form, or entry on the CT600 Return or computations, is required. The following further guidance is provided to help reply to companies who request information about claiming the relief.

IM1142f : World Health Organisation Guidelines

The legislation requires not simply that the medical supplies or equipment concerned are given for human use, but in addition that the gift is made 'for humanitarian purposes'. This further condition reflects the broad intention of the provisions, which is to encourage responsible and appropriate donations.

The World Health Organisation produces Guidelines for Drug Donations. They are accessible at www.who.int/medicines/library/par/who-edm-par-99-4/who-edm-par-99-4.doc.

Cases which fall within the WHO Guidelines should be accepted as meeting the condition that the gift is made for humanitarian purposes. If the circumstances of the case give any reason for doubting that the gift was made for humanitarian purposes, advice should be sought from Business Tax 1/2, Room 4E7, 4th Floor, 22 Kingsway, London, WC2B 6NR.

IM1142g : definitions

The term "medical supplies and medical equipment" should be interpreted broadly. All medicines or vaccines for human use are included. "Equipment" includes

- equipment required for the delivery and administration of medicines e.g. syringes; and

- other equipment appropriate to the situation such as bandages, medical appliances; and

- preventative equipment such as mosquito nets.

IM1142h : effective date

The relief applies to gifts made on or after 1st April 2002.'

---

13   Close Companies

13.6   **Exceptions: 'recognised stock exchanges'.** It is noted that a further Revenue Press Release (27 November 2002) sets out a new approach to the recognition of overseas stock exchanges for tax law purposes, as follows.

'**Introduction**

1 The application of tax provisions to shares and securities is frequently determined by whether the shares or securities are "listed on a recognised stock exchange" or by another phrase or expression which includes the words "recognised stock exchange".

13 Close Companies

2 The Inland Revenue keeps a list of "recognised stock exchanges" for tax purposes (available at www.inlandrevenue.gov.uk). However, recent developments in the international financial services industry, including the creation of new types of stock exchanges and internationally-oriented exchanges in offshore financial centres, have made it harder to decide which overseas exchanges should be recognised for tax purposes.

3 Inland Revenue has therefore been reviewing its policy on the recognition of stock exchanges and is now announcing a new approach to designating recognised stock exchanges. This is expected to result in an increase in the number of overseas stock exchanges recognised for tax purposes.

Details

4 The Inland Revenue has the power under section 841 of the Income and Corporation Taxes Act 1988 to designate recognised stock exchanges overseas for the purposes of the Tax Acts.

5 The purpose of this power is to facilitate the interpretation of various provisions in tax law which use the concept of a recognised stock exchange. Recognition by the Inland Revenue of a stock exchange confers no other status on the exchange concerned; it does not constitute any form of recognition or approval of the exchange for regulatory or other purposes nor does it provide any form of approval or recommendation of any of the investments which are listed or traded on that exchange.

6 The Inland Revenue has been reviewing its approach towards the recognition of stock exchanges and the policy and criteria it should adopt in deciding whether or not an exchange should be recognised. It has concluded, in the light of developments in the international financial services industry and in the regulation of that industry, that it should follow a more broadly based approach which is likely to result in the recognition of a larger number of stock exchanges outside the UK.

7 The Inland Revenue will in future consider the following matters when deciding whether or not an overseas stock exchange should be designated as a recognised stock exchange for UK tax purposes:

- is the stock exchange undertaking the normal business of a stock exchange and regulated as an investment exchange in a major economy or a significant international financial centre;

- has the jurisdiction concerned proper and effective arrangements for financial regulation which meet internationally accepted modern standards in this area; and

- is there any objection on wider public policy grounds to the recognition for tax purposes of the exchange, or of exchanges in that jurisdiction.

Background

8 Section 841 of the Income and Corporation Taxes Act 1988 defines a recognised stock exchange for tax purposes as the (London) Stock Exchange and any such exchange outside the United Kingdom as is approved by an Order of the Board of Inland Revenue. Over the years, a large number of overseas exchanges have been recognised. The current list of recognised stock exchanges overseas is available on the Revenue website (www.inlandrevenue.gov.uk).

9 Current Inland Revenue policy is to consider recognition of stock exchanges on receipt of a request from the exchange concerned. So the fact that an exchange is not included in the list of recognised stock exchanges may simply mean that it has not sought recognition.'

13A   Clubs and Societies

13A.8   **Community amateur sports clubs.** It is noted that a list of registered clubs is published on the Revenue website at www.inlandrevenue.gov.uk/casc/registered_clubs.pdf.

Also, as regards 'qualifying purposes' in relation to tax reliefs for such clubs, the following note is added.

'*SI 2002 No 1966* designates the eligible sports for these purposes as those appearing on the list of activities recognised by the various National Sports Councils (which is available on the Sport England website at www.sportengland.org/gateway/recognised_activities.htm).'

14   Community Investment Tax Relief

14.1   **Introduction.** It is noted that, by virtue of *SI 2003 No 88*, the appointed day for the commencement of relief is confirmed as 17 April 2002, and that for the making of claims as 22 January 2003, and that *SI 2003 No 96* makes provision for the accreditation of CDFIs.

It is also noted that the European Commission has determined that the scheme is outside the scope of, or compatible with, EU state aid rules.

17   Construction Industry Tax Scheme

17.2   **Payments from which tax must be deducted.** It is noted that a new Revenue Pamphlet IR 180(CIS) deals with the application of the scheme to non-residents.

17.3   **Registration cards.** It is noted that, by virtue of *SI 2002 No 2225, regs 3–5*, registration cards may now be renewed, and temporary cards may have a maximum validity of 12 months (or, in exceptional cases where the issuer deems it appropriate, 36 months).

17.4   **Sub-contractors' tax certificates.** A reference is added to the case of *Shaw v Vicky Construction Ltd Ch D, [2002] STC 1544*, in which a company (V) which was granted a tax certificate under *ICTA 1988, s 561* for a period of 12 months in July 2000 applied in July 2001 for the certificate to be renewed. The Revenue rejected the claim, on the grounds that V had not met its 'compliance obligation', as it had persistently paid its PAYE liabilities at least a month after the due date. V appealed, contending that its failure to pay its PAYE was 'minor and technical', within *section 565(4)*, and that there was no reason to doubt that it would comply with its obligations. The Ch D rejected this contention and held that the Revenue were entitled to reject the application. Ferris J held that V's non-compliance was not 'minor and technical' and 'gave rise to real doubt whether there would be due compliance in the future'. Furthermore, the refusal to renew the certificate did not give rise to any breach of the *European Convention on Human Rights*.

17.7   **Administration.** It is noted that amendments are made to the administrative arrangements for the operation of the scheme by *SI 2002 No 2225* and *SI 2003 No 536*. The first two paragraphs are now as follows.

'Detailed administrative arrangements for the operation of the scheme are contained in *The Income Tax (Sub-contractors in the Construction Industry) Regulations 1993 (SI 1993 No 743)* as amended by the *(Amendment) Regulations 1998 (SI 1998 No 2622)*, *1999 (SI 1999*

No 825), 2000 (SI 2000 No 2742), 2002 (SI 2002 No 2225) and *2003 (SI 2003 No 536).* The arrangements for accounting for deductions and for interest on unpaid or overpaid tax (see *SI 1993 No 743, regs 8-19; SI 1998 No 2622, regs 9, 10; SI 1999 No 825, reg 2; SI 2000 No 1151; SI 2003 No 536, regs 4–6*) broadly follow those for PAYE (see Tolley's Income Tax under Pay As You Earn and Revenue Pamphlet IR 14/15(CIS), chapter 6), and there are detailed provisions governing the form and use of sub-contractor's tax certificates (see *SI 1993 No 743, reg 24, Sch 1; SI 1998 No 2622, regs 18, 38; SI 1999 No 2159, reg 10; SI 2002 No 2225, reg 6*) and the requirements for contractors' end of year returns of all payments to sub-contractors (see *SI 1993 No 743, reg 40A; SI 1998 No 2622, reg 33*). See also below under *Failure to deduct and under-deduction.* The Inland Revenue have powers to inspect records of contractors and sub-contractors (see *SI 1993 No 743, regs 41, 41A; SI 1998 No 2622, reg 34; SI 1999 No 2159, reg 8; SI 2003 No 536, reg 7*). Further regulations may be made by statutory instrument. [*ICTA 1988, s 566; FA 1995, Sch 27 para 9; FA 1998, Sch 8 para 6*]. See Revenue Pamphlet IR 109 as regards negotiation of settlements. The Revenue have published a Code of Practice (No 3, available from local tax offices) setting out their standards for the way in which inspections of contractors' records are conducted and the rights and responsibilities of taxpayers.

Contractors are able to submit some of the vouchers information using electronic data interchange ("EDI"). [*SI 1993 No 743, reg 7(4)(b), reg 37A(2)(b), reg 40A(9)(b), reg 44A, reg 44B; SI 1998 No 2622, regs 7(4)(5), 29, 33, 35; SI 2003 No 536, reg 8*]. Full details should have been sent to all known contractors and sub-contractors by the end of 1998. For an outline of how EDI may be used, see Revenue Press Release 1 September 1998.'

---

18   Controlled Foreign Companies

18.1   **Introduction.** It is noted that the Revenue Guidance Notes on the CFC provisions are now available on the Revenue website at www.inlandrevenue.gov.uk/ctsafc/pgn.pdf.

18.11   **Exceptions.** It is noted that *SI 1998 No 3081 (The Controlled Foreign Companies (Excluded Countries) Regulations 1998)* has been amended, in particular by *SI 2002 No 2406,* which removes Ireland from the list of excluded countries.

In relation to 18.11(vi) (the 'motive test'), a reference is added to the case of *Association of British Travel Agents Ltd v CIR (Sp C 359), [2003] SSCD 194,* in which the Revenue issued a number of directions to ABTA, applying the CFC legislation of *ICTA 1988, s 747 et seq.* to the profits of two captive insurance companies for the periods from 1 July 1996 to 30 June 1999. ABTA appealed, contending that the effect of *section 748(3)* was that no apportionment should be made, since it was not 'one of the main reasons for the company's existence in that period to achieve a reduction in United Kingdom tax by a diversion of profits from the United Kingdom'. The Special Commissioners reviewed the evidence in detail, rejected this contention, and dismissed ABTA's appeal. The Commissioners held that the transactions satisfied the requirements of *section 748(3)(a),* holding that the tax reductions which ABTA had actually achieved were 'an effect of the transaction' and were 'not one of the main purposes that ABTA was trying to achieve'. However, the Commissioners also held that ABTA failed to satisfy the requirements of *section 748(3)(b),* observing that *section 748(3)(b)* 'accepts the genuineness of the transaction but considers whether the reason for the existence of non-resident entity (*sic*) was the reduction in tax caused by its being non-resident, and therefore concentrates on whether the same result could have been achieved using a UK-resident vehicle'. On the evidence, one of the main reasons why ABTA had chosen to use captive insurance companies, rather than an in-house fund, 'was to achieve the tax reduction by the diversion of profits between the existence of the captives and the other alternatives'.

The Commissioners observed that 'a UK-resident captive would achieve exactly the same result without the tax benefits'.

Also in relation to the motive test, the guidelines listed at (A)–(J) (and the preceding paragraph) are revised as follows.

'The Revenue Notes referred to at 18.1 above originally contained guidelines on the application of the "motive test" at (vi) above. These have now been replaced with separate notes on the motive test, which are available on the Revenue website at www.inlandrevenue.gov.uk/ctsacfc/motive_test_guidance.pdf. These are designated INTM208010 to INTM208350, although the significance of these identifiers is not clear at the time of writing. The following points are of particular interest.

(A)   The motive test is entirely separate from the tests at (i) to (v) above, and failure to satisfy those other tests will not prejudice consideration of the motive test, except that where there is a marginal and isolated failure to satisfy those other tests this is regarded as an indication that the CFC is not being used to reduce tax liabilities (INTM208170, INTM208180).

(B)   In determining what the tax position would have been had a transaction not been carried out, hypothetical transactions which might have taken place instead are not taken into account (INTM208070).

(C)   Tax consequences remote from the transaction are not regarded as resulting from it (e.g. a fee received for giving tax planning advice to an unconnected UK resident would not lead to failure of the motive test merely because that person achieved a tax reduction by acting on that advice) (INTM208060).

(D)   A reduction in tax which is substantial in absolute terms will not be regarded as 'minimal' merely because it represents a relatively small proportion of the total liability of the company concerned (INTM208070).

(E)   The motives of a CFC's customers have no relevance to the motive test (INTM208080).

(F)   As regards (1) above, it would be rare for this not to apply, as it is unlikely that a group would allow the diversion of receipts within the group to an outsider, and any claim that the law of the territory in which the CFC is resident would prevent a UK company from acquiring the CFC's receipts 'would have to be looked at very carefully' (INTM208140).

(G)   The transfer of the activities of an overseas branch to a non-resident subsidiary will often be made for predominantly commercial reasons, e.g. as a necessary preliminary to expanding the overseas business or attracting local capital, and in such cases the motive test will often be satisfied as tax considerations will normally be only a subsidiary reason for the transfer. The Revenue will, however, wish to consider in depth the reasons for incorporation (INTM208200).

(H)   The Revenue will, on receipt of a satisfactory clearance application (see above), accept that the motive test is satisfied in the case of newly-acquired overseas subsidiaries up to the end of the first full twelve-month accounting period following acquisition. This applies only to CFCs not previously under UK control and whose main business remained unchanged throughout the period in question (INTM208210).

(I)   The UK holder of an interest in a CFC may also be treated as having a creditor relationship with the CFC (see 44.2 LOAN RELATIONSHIPS). Where this is so and the increase in value under the loan relationships provisions reflects the chargeable profits arising for an accounting period, the motive test is accepted as applying for that period. This is because the reduction in UK tax is fully compensated for by the tax charge on the UK parent, indicating that the achievement of that reduction is not a main reason for the CFC's existence (INTM208270).

For the circumstances in which holding companies (and in particular "brass plate" holding companies) may satisfy the motive test, see INTM208220 *et seq.*.

A number of examples of different aspects of the motive test are included at INTM208280 to INTM208350.'

18.14   **Exempt activities.** As regards paragraph (1)(*b*), it is noted that legislation is to be introduced in the 2003 Finance Bill to extend the persons from whom no more than 50% of gross trading receipts may be derived to include persons not already so included who are either UK-resident companies, non-UK resident companies carrying on business through a UK branch or agency (by reference only to receipts derived from that branch or agency) or individuals habitually resident in the UK (although this extended definition is *not* to apply to certain CFCs engaged in insurance business). Corresponding amendments are to be made to *ICTA 1988, Sch 25 para 11*. Revenue Press Release 27 November 2002 is referred to in this respect.

Also, the paragraph on the definition of '*resident*' is revised as follows.

'"*Resident*" in this context is as defined in 18.3 above. However, in the case of a non-UK resident company which, for the accounting period in question, is not liable to tax in any territory by reason of domicile, residence or place of management, but whose affairs are "effectively managed" in a territory outside the UK in which companies are not liable to tax by reason of domicile, residence or place of management, then it is treated for this purpose as resident in the latter territory or, if there is more than one, in such a territory as is notified to the Board for this purpose by the UK resident company or companies having a majority interest in the CFC (see 18.9(iv) above). Where, however, the territory in which it is "effectively managed" is either the Hong Kong or the Macao Special Administrative Region of the People's Republic of China, and it is liable to tax for the period in that Region, legislation is to be introduced in the Finance Bill 2003 requiring it to be treated as resident in that Region (see Revenue Press Release 27 November 2002).'

19   Corporate Venturing Scheme

19.1   **Introduction.** It is noted that the new Revenue Venture Capital Schemes Manual ('VCM') has been published, dealing *inter alia* with the Corporate Venturing Scheme. A general cross-reference to VCM 10000–17320, VCM 50000 *et seq.* is inserted. Other references to the Inspector's Manual ('IM') in this chapter are accordingly amended to the corresponding reference in the new Manual. These are as follows.

Paragraph	Old reference	New reference
19.6	IM 6723, IM 6982	VCM 15070, VCM 50140
	IM 6723, IM 6983	VCM 17040, VCM 50140
19.8	IM 6701	VCM 50020
	IM 6703, IM 6975A	VCM 12080, VCM 50030

19.6   **Qualifying issuing company: trading activities requirement.** See introductory note at the head of the chapter.

19.7   **Qualifying trades.** As regards the definition of 'substantial' in relation to the carrying on of excluded activities, the following note is substituted.

'As regards (iii) above, "substantial" is not defined, but where, judged by any measure which is reasonable in the circumstances (normally turnover or capital employed), excluded activities account for less than 20% of the activities of the trade as a whole, the Revenue do not regard them as amounting to a "substantial" part of the trade. (Revenue Venture Capital Trusts Manual, VCM 17040).'

19.8   **General requirements.** See introductory note at the head of the chapter.

19.9   **Advance clearance.** It is noted that the address to which applications for clearance should be sent is now Revenue Policy, Business Tax, Corporate Venturing Scheme Unit, Central Correspondence Unit, Room M26, New Wing, Somerset House, London WC2R 1LB.

20   Distributions

20.8   **Interest and other distributions.** A reference is added to the possible impact of the case of *Lankhorst-Hohorst GmbH v Finanzamt Steinfurt CJEC Case C-324/00* on the legislation referred to in 20.6 and 20.7 above. German corporation tax legislation contains a provision requiring payment of interest on debts due from parent companies to be recategorised as a 'covert distribution of profits' when the relevant loan capital is 'more than three times the shareholder's proportional equity capital at any point in the financial year, save where the company limited by shares could have obtained the loan capital from a third party under otherwise similar circumstances or the loan capital constitutes borrowing to finance normal banking transactions'. A German subsidiary of a Netherlands company appealed against corporation tax assessments, contending that the relevant legislation contravened *Article 43EC* of the *EC Treaty*. The CJEC accepted this contention, holding that *Article 43EC* precluded the measure in question. The CJEC observed that the relevant legislation 'does not have the specific purpose of preventing wholly artificial arrangements, designed to circumvent German tax legislation, but applies generally to any situation ion which the parent company has its seat, for whatever reason, outside the Federal Republic of Germany'.

20.17   **Effect of distribution.** A reference is added to the case of *Strand Futures and Options Ltd v Vojak Ch D, [2003] STC 331*, in which, in 1995, a company (C) purchased 89,700 of its own shares from another company (S). S appealed against a corporation tax assessment for the relevant period, contending that the effect of *ICTA 1988, s 208* was that the consideration should not be treated as chargeable to corporation tax. The Ch D accepted this contention and allowed the appeal (reversing the Special Commissioners' decision). Etherton J held that *section 208* 'exempts from corporation tax all distributions of a company, whether as income or as giving rise to a capital gain'. Accordingly, the sale by S to C did not give rise to any corporation tax liability.

21   Double Tax Relief

21.3   **Relief by agreement.** A reference is added to an article in the Revenue Tax Bulletin (December 2002 pp 989–991), reproduced below, concerning the circumstances in which the Revenue will certify that a company is UK resident for the purposes of double tax agreements.

'CERTIFICATES OF UK RESIDENCE FOR COMPANIES

1. This article explains the circumstances in which the Inland Revenue will certify that a company is a resident of the United Kingdom for the purpose of double taxation agreements (DTAs) entered into by the UK. It does not consider the position of individuals.

Residence as a condition in DTAs for obtaining relief from tax

2. The relevant DTA should always be considered in a particular case. But the following is the general pattern under the UK's DTAs.

3. A company may claim relief from another State's tax under the DTA between the UK and that State only if it meets one or more conditions. The first is that the company is "a resident of the UK" for the purpose of the DTA in question.

4. Under Article 4(1) of a typical DTA a company will be a resident of the UK if, under the laws of the UK, it is liable to tax in the UK by reason of its domicile, residence, place of management, place of incorporation or any other criterion of a similar nature.

5. A company that is incorporated in the UK is resident here under domestic law (Section 66 FA 1988) unless

- it migrated with Treasury consent before 15 March 1988, continues to carry on a business and is centrally managed and controlled outside the UK; or

- it is treated as not resident in the UK by virtue of Section 249 FA 1994 (under which a company is treated as non-resident if it is so treated for the purposes of a DTA — see paragraphs 22–24 below).

6. Being a resident of the UK may be the only general condition for claiming relief from the tax of another State, eg if the company has manufacturing or retailing profits and it does not have in the other State a permanent establishment, as defined in the DTA, to which the profits are attributable.

7. But if the company derives dividends, interest or royalties from the other State, then another condition will usually have to be met. This is that the company is either the beneficial owner of the income in question, or is subject to tax in the UK in respect of the income. Some DTAs have both tests.

Examining claims under DTAs

8. The Inland Revenue can be expected to take reasonable steps to support companies that are residents of the UK in their legitimate claims to relief from the tax of another State with which the UK has entered into a DTA; just as companies that are residents of the other State will expect the tax authorities of that State to support them in their legitimate claims to relief from UK tax under the DTA.

9. If a UK company claims relief from the tax of another State under the DTA between the UK and that State, the other State will verify that the conditions for relief are met and will ask appropriate questions if the position is not immediately clear.

10. However, the Inland Revenue must take reasonable precautions against statements made by it being used to obtain relief from another State's tax if that relief is not due. It is important that we do not jeopardise our relations with other States. We have a responsibility to the generality of UK taxpayers to maintain the UK's reputation in this area.

11. We will therefore, as necessary, ask a company for information that we need to verify the accuracy of statements that we are asked to make in support of its claim to relief from another State's tax under a DTA. And we will not support a claim to relief where we have information which shows that the claim may not be valid.

12. For example, having regard to paragraphs 6 and 7 above, a residence certificate will not be given if the profits or income in question are not profits or income of the UK company concerned. This will be the case if, for example, it acts as an agent for another person rather than as principal. We have also seen cases where a UK company has lent its name to a transaction when the beneficial owner of the profits or income resulting from that transaction is a different person.

13. It would be wrong for us to certify the residence status of a UK-incorporated company if the certificate is likely to be used to support a claim to relief from another State's tax in such circumstances, since the proper person to claim such relief is the person who is the beneficial owner of the income. This would be the case even if the UK company was rewarded by the other person, for example by a payment of commission or for the use of its name, since this would not be the income that was the subject of the claim under the DTA. It would also be wrong to certify UK residence if we have insufficient information to form a view on whether the profits or income concerned are profits or income of the UK company or not.

Certifying that a company is UK resident

14. If we are asked to certify that a company is UK resident, we will need to know the use to which such a certificate will be put before providing it.

15. For example, if a company requires a letter simply confirming that it is registered with the Inland Revenue in order to be allowed to do business in another State, the person dealing with the company's affairs can provide a letter stating that they are dealt with in his or her office. Such a letter should make it clear that it is not a certificate of UK residence, since this is not relevant to the company's request.

16. However, a company might want to use a certificate of UK residence in order to claim relief, under the DTA between the UK and another State, from tax that would otherwise be payable in that State.

17. The person dealing with the company's affairs will normally first check the Double Taxation Relief Manual to see if the other State has provided a form for claiming relief from its tax on the income in question. This may be the case especially with dividends, interest and royalties.

18. If the Manual indicates that such a form exists, the company must make its claim using it and, as appropriate, ask the Inland Revenue to certify its residence status on the form. The other State will have designed the form with the intention that it should be used in relation to the types of income in question, and we will not undermine its administrative procedures by providing a letter certifying UK residence instead.

19. But if the other State does not provide a form for use in the circumstances of the case, the company might ask for a letter certifying that the company is a resident of the UK for the purposes of the DTA.

20. In either situation, for the reasons given in paragraphs 10–13 we must be sure that the Inland Revenue does not support a claim to relief that could not be justified. A company requesting a letter certifying UK residence should provide details of the nature of the proposed transaction and the income concerned. If they are not provided, we will normally ask for them. We will also check the relevant DTA to make sure that there is no obvious reason why the company could not claim the relief. We will not certify UK residence if we think that to do so could mislead the other State into thinking that the Inland Revenue believes that the relief is due if this is not the case.

21. It should usually, for example in the case of established companies whose tax affairs are well known to us, be possible to certify that a UK-incorporated company that is clearly the beneficial owner of the income that is the subject of the claim under the DTA (and/or, depending on the terms of the DTA, is subject to tax in the UK in respect of the income) is a resident of the UK for the purpose of claiming relief under the DTA in respect of that income.

22. However, it should not be overlooked that the company, even though UK-incorporated, could also be resident in another State under that State's domestic law. Such a company would then be dually resident. If there is a DTA between the UK and the other State it may contain a tie-breaker test, stating typically that a company that is a resident of both States

37

under their respective domestic laws shall, for the purposes of the DTA between them, be deemed to be a resident only of the State in which its place of effective management is situated. Where this is situated is a question of fact.

23. If the company's place of effective management is in the other State, it would not then be regarded as a resident of the UK for the purposes of the DTA between the UK and that State. And (except for the purposes of the controlled foreign company rules in certain situations — Section 747(1B) ICTA 1988, inserted by FA 2002) under Section 249 FA 1994 the company would not be regarded as resident in the UK under domestic law either. Consequently it would not be a resident of the UK for the purposes of any other DTA that the UK has entered into.

24. The lack, or limited extent, of presence or activities in the UK might be an indication that the company is effectively managed outside the UK, and that it is therefore a dual resident company, with the consequences described above. If a UK-incorporated company does not seem to have much or any presence or activities in the UK, we will not certify that the company is a resident of the UK for the purposes of domestic law or of a DTA if we

• have reasonable grounds for believing that the company may be effectively managed in, and hence may be resident in, a State other than the UK with which the UK has a DTA with a tie-breaker test for dual resident companies; or

• have insufficient information to make a decision one way or the other.

25. With regard to the first of those points, the residence status of the company's directors (including shadow directors) and the ultimate beneficial shareholders may be a matter about which we properly seek information in this connection.

26. A company seeking a certificate of UK residence should, however, be able to provide sufficient information to show where it is effectively managed if we ask about the point. Revenue Policy, International (Company Residence) can, if required, provide advice and guidance in applying the established facts in particular cases to the tie-breaker wording in any DTA.

27. With regard to the second of the points in paragraph 24, all we can reasonably certify is that the company is incorporated in the UK but that we are unable to confirm its residence status for purposes of DTAs concluded by the UK.

Exchange of information

28. If the person dealing with a company's affairs has information about its connections with, or business dealings in, another State that he or she thinks may be of interest to that State, he or she will arrange for that information to be sent to the other State using the prescribed competent authority procedures, according to the terms of the exchange of information Article in the UK's DTA with that State or, where appropriate, under the EC Mutual Assistance Directive (paragraphs 350 onwards of the Double Taxation Relief Manual). Information will be sent spontaneously as well as at the request of the other State. This will include cases where a certificate of residence has been provided and it is subsequently claimed, or it becomes clear, that the transaction in respect of which it was given did not take place.'

Also, in relation to dividends, a reference is added to an article in the Revenue Tax Bulletin (February 2003 p 1007), reproduced below, following up that in the August 2001 edition (pp 870–874), concerning the application of *ICTA 1988, s 803A*.

'DOUBLE TAXATION RELIEF: UNDERLYING TAX: TAX CONSOLIDATIONS FALLING WITHIN SECTION 803A OF ICTA 1988

Tax Bulletin 57, published in January 2002, gave details of tax consolidations for a number of countries which brought companies within Section 803A of the Income and Corporation

Taxes Act 1988. This section aggregates relevant profits and tax for the purposes of calculating the rate of underlying tax that is attributable to a dividend where a number of companies have been taxed as a single, consolidated entity in another country.

The Australian Government has recently enacted a tax consolidation regime effective from 1 January 2003 under which wholly owned groups of Australian-resident companies are able to consolidate. The holding company and each member of the group will be jointly and severally liable to pay the group tax liability except where there is a tax sharing agreement. In that case, the agreement will determine the contribution each member makes towards the group tax liability. In either case, the companies will be within Section 803A for the purposes of calculating underlying tax relief.

Under Section 803A the relevant profits for any year are the group profits arising in that year so that inter-company dividends in that year are ignored. The exception is where the foreign holding company receives a dividend paid from a subsidiary's profits arising before the tax consolidation came into effect. In that case, the dividend should be added to the group relevant profits and the associated underlying tax (calculated on the basis of the paying company's own profits and tax) should be added to the group tax. That will ensure that profits and tax do not fall out of account on the transition from a company to a group basis.

Contact Points

Further advice in a particular case may be obtained from

Paul West
Revenue Policy International (Underlying Tax Group)
Fitz Roy House
PO Box 46
Nottingham
NG2 1BD

Tel: 0115 974 2020

Or more general policy advice from

Susan New
Revenue Policy International (External Relations Group)
Victory House
30-34 Kingsway
London
WC2B 6ES

Tel: 020 7438 7250

E-mail: Susan.New@ir.gsi.gov.uk'

21.10   **Agreements in force.** It is noted that new agreements with South Africa (*SI 2003 No 3138*) and Taiwan (*SI 2003 No 3137*) came into force with effect from 1 April 2003 (UK) and 1 January 2003 (South Africa and Taiwan).

It is also noted that the commencement of the agreement with Lithuania is subject to ratification of the protocol published as *SI 2002 No 2847*.

It is further noted that the new agreement with the USA (*SI 2002 No 2848*) is not yet in force, but that *SI 1946 No 1331*, *SI 1955 No 499*, *SI 1961 No 985*, *SI 1980 No 779*, *SI 1994 No 1418* and *SI 1996 No 1781* are all revoked from 1 January 2001 by *SI 2000 No 3330*.

Additionally, a new note on USA is added and the notes on China and the USSR revised as follows.

'*China.* The Convention published as *SI 1984 No 1826* does not apply to the Hong Kong or Macao Special Administrative Regions. (Revenue Tax Bulletin October 1996 p 357). See above as regards Hong Kong Air Transport and Shipping agreements.

USA. It is understood that the new agreement will take effect in the UK from 1 April 2003 and in the USA from 1 January 2004 (1 May 2003 in both the UK and the USA in respect of tax withheld at source). For an article setting out the understanding of the Revenue on how certain of the provisions of the new USA treaty will be interpreted and applied, see Revenue Tax Bulletin Special Edition April 2003.

USSR. Following the dissolution of the USSR, new agreements have come into force with Azerbaijan, Estonia, Kazakhstan, Latvia, Lithuania (subject to protocol), the Russian Federation, Ukraine and Uzbekistan (see above). *SI 1986 No 224* (the former USSR agreement) is treated as continuing to apply to Belarus, Tajikistan and Turkmenistan (in the case of Belarus until the coming into force of *SI 1995 No 2706*). It was similarly so treated by the UK until 31 March 2002 in the case of Armenia, Georgia, Kyrgyzstan, Lithuania and Moldova (none of which considered itself bound by that convention) but as ceasing so to apply after that date (although new treaties are in force with Lithuania (subject to protocol) and under negotiation with Georgia). (Revenue Pamphlet IR 131, SP 4/01, 19 December 2001 as revised).'

23   Exchange Gains and Losses

23.3   **Revenue practice.** This section is revised as follows.

'**Revenue practice.** Following the decision in the *Marine Midland* case (see 23.2 above), the Revenue issued a Statement of Practice (Revenue Pamphlet IR 131, SP 1/87, 17 February 1987) setting out their views on the general treatment of exchange differences for tax purposes. These are summarised at 23.4 below. Following the introduction of the *FA 1993* provisions described at 23.5 *et seq.* below, which applied to "qualifying companies" for accounting periods beginning after 22 March 1995, SP 1/87 continued to apply to non-qualifying companies and to individuals and partnerships. For accounting periods beginning on or after 1 October 2002, the *FA 1993* provisions are repealed (see 23.5 below), and exchange gains and losses of *all* companies within the charge to corporation tax are brought within the LOAN RELATIONSHIPS (44) or FINANCIAL INSTRUMENTS AND DERIVATIVE CONTRACTS (25) rules. Statement of Practice SP 1/87 accordingly ceases to apply to companies within the charge to corporation tax, and is replaced by Statement of Practice SP 2/02, 30 September 2002, which continues to apply to other persons carrying on a trade (see Tolley's Income Tax under Schedule D, Cases I and II — Exchange Gains and Losses).

Simon's Direct Tax Service. See **B3.1708.**'

23.4   **Statement of Practice SP 1/87.** In the closing **Note**, it is confirmed that the draft revised SP 1/87 has been published as Statement of Practice SP 2/02, 30 September 2002, and does not apply to companies within the charge to corporation tax.

23.5   **FA 1993 provisions for qualifying companies.** It is noted that the draft *Exchange Gains and Losses (Savings, Transitional Provisions and Consequential Amendments) Regulations 2002* have now been published as *SI 2002 No 1969.*

23.32   **Commencement and transitional provisions.** It is noted that the draft *Exchange Gains and Losses (Savings, Transitional Provisions and Consequential Amendments) Regulations 2002* and *Exchange Gains and Losses (Bringing into Account Gains or Losses) Regulations 2002* have now been published as, respectively, *SI 2002 No 1969* and *SI 2002 No 1970.*

25   Financial Instruments and Derivative Contracts

25.10   **Derivative contracts rules: special computational provisions.** It is noted that the draft revised SP 3/95 has been published as Statement of Practice SP 4/02, 30 September 2002.

25.11   **Derivative contracts rules: authorised unit trusts and open-ended investment companies.** The following note is added.

'For a statement agreed between the Revenue and the Investment Management Association confirming the tax treatment in these circumstances, see Revenue Tax Bulletin August 2002 pp 948–950.'

The Revenue Tax Bulletin article referred to is reproduced below.

'AUTHORISED UNIT TRUSTS (AUTS) AND OPEN-ENDED INVESTMENT COMPANIES (OEICS)

New Loan Relationships and Derivative Contract regimes

This statement has been agreed between the Investment Management Association (IMA) and the Inland Revenue to confirm the tax treatment of AUTs and OEICs which invest in Loan Relationships and Derivative Contracts following the introduction of the Finance Act 2002.

The new provisions extend the previous exemption for profits arising from derivative contracts. This statement is intended to remove any possible uncertainty arising from the new provisions and to explain the rules under which tax exemption will continue, thereby enabling funds to invest in these instruments with certainty as to their tax treatment.

Background

1) AUTs and OEICs are included in the revised loan relationships and derivative contract regimes that will come into force for all accounting periods beginning on or after 1 October 2002. The revised loan relationships regime also broadly assimilates provision for taxing foreign exchange gains.

2) These are important changes for the sector. Previously AUTs and OEICs were only within loan relationships in respect of their debtor relationships (liabilities). And they were not "qualifying companies" for the purposes of the old financial instruments or foreign exchange rules.

3) Reform will ease the compliance burden for managers of AUTs and OEICs when preparing their tax computations, because the tax treatment of the funds will now be more closely aligned with fund accounting. Much of the complexity associated with the old rules, including the application of the accrued income scheme, will be removed. The new arrangements are also expected to be complementary, and more responsive, to commercial and regulatory change.

4) In general, the new rules make no distinction for most companies between the taxation of capital and revenue profits from loan relationships or derivative contracts. But authorised funds are to be treated differently.

5) This is because AUTs and OEICs are exempt from corporation tax on their capital gains. The underlying policy is that the capital profits of AUTs and OEICs should not be taxed (or their capital losses relieved), either under the new Schedule or under any other provision.

6) Bringing AUTs and OEICs into the new regime has also meant that some existing special provisions that applied to them can be repealed, in particular, section 468AA and Paragraph 1(2)(c) Schedule 5AA ICTA 1988, which prevented the taxation as income of certain profits from futures and options contracts.

25 Financial Instruments and Derivative Contracts

7) The following 'Q&A' explain how the new rules work in relation to AUTs and OEICs and cover the main practical implications of reform.

"Capital Profits"

How do the new rules define those profits that are not taxable?

8) The legislation provides that "capital profits and losses" from the creditor (asset) loan relationships of AUTs and OEICs and their derivative contracts must not be taxed or relieved as credits or debits respectively. The treatment of AUT and OEIC debtor (liability) loan relationships remains the same.

9) If, in accordance with a relevant Statement of Recommended Practice (SORP), an AUT or OEIC properly accounts for creditor loan relationship and derivative contract profits or losses under either of the two headings,

- "net gains/losses on investments" or

- "other gains/losses",

those profits or losses will be treated as "capital profits and losses". As such the appropriate accounting treatment will govern whether or not a profit is taxable.

What is a relevant SORP in this context?

10) The current SORP is, for AUTs, the SORP issued by Investment Management Regulatory Organisation (IMRO) in January 1997 and, for OEICs, the SORP issued by the Financial Services Authority (FSA) in November 2000. Responsibility as SORP making body for collective investment schemes is expected to pass to IMA, which intends to combine and update the existing SORPs.

11) Where an AUT or OEIC is either required or permitted to use a different SORP in the future, the new rules provide for the tax treatment to link to that SORP as well.

The new rules include regulating powers for the Treasury to change the definition of "capital profits and losses". Why are they needed?

12) As the legislation is linked to the language and definitions of the relevant SORPs, it might be necessary to respond quickly to changes in those SORPs. It would most likely be impracticable to make the necessary changes by primary legislation so provision for secondary legislation is needed. The rules are clear that the regulation powers can only be used when changes are made to a SORP which an authorised fund is required or permitted to follow.

Repeal of section 468AA ICTA 1988

Section 468AA ICTA 1988 provided that profits of an AUT or OEIC from futures and options could not be taxed as trading income. Does its repeal signal an intention to argue that certain authorised funds are trading in respect of their derivative contracts; and, in particular, will the Revenue seek to tax capital returns?

13) No. The repeal of section 468AA has no impact on this in practice.

14) Further, while it is impossible to say, in advance of a transaction taking place, that it is not going to be a trading transaction, the general and prevailing assumption is that authorised funds will not be conducting a trade. They are investment vehicles and are regulated as such.

15) Section 468AA has been repealed because it is no longer necessary and because its retention might in fact create distortions in tax treatment. Where a fund returns a profit from a derivative contract that is to be dealt with under the new Schedule, that profit can only be taxed under the rules of the Schedule. So if the profit is a "capital profit", it cannot be taken into account as a taxable credit. There is no question of it being taxable under any other provisions, including Case I of Schedule D. This follows from the provisions of paragraph 1 and 32(1) (AUTs) and 33(1)(OEICs) Finance Act 2002.

16) This treatment will cover the majority of derivative contracts held by an authorised fund. In fact, because the new rules for derivative contracts are drawn more widely than the financial instruments legislation, funds should have greater certainty about their tax treatment. Section 468AA only gave Case I exemption for futures and options, but that exemption now goes further. A number of capital returns that were previously not exempt from tax are now exempted, including those on certain derivative contracts which did not previously enjoy exemption under section 468AA.

17) Even if a derivative contract is otherwise excluded because of the nature of its underlying subject matter, and the relevant contract is entered into for trading purposes, any resultant profit or loss will normally be subject to the rules of the Schedule.

18) If, in such cases, profits are returned as income and are therefore taxable credits under the Schedule, the retention of section 468AA is contradictory. It makes no sense to exempt something under one rule yet tax it under another.

19) The overall effect therefore is that where profits are properly accounted for as "capital profits", they will not be taxable. The exemption applies to all contracts within the new regime and it is not open to the Revenue to tax (under Schedule D Case 1 as trading profits or under any other provision apart from Schedule 26) capital profits which arise from them and are properly accounted for as such.

What will happen to profits from those derivative contracts that are not dealt with by the new Schedule?

20) In terms of relevance to section 468AA repeal, the derivative contracts affected would only be those over land, tangible movable property (other than commodities which are tangible assets) and intangible fixed assets. Where profits from such contracts are properly accounted for as "capital profits", which would be the expected accounting treatment, the existing protection provided by section 100(1) TCGA 1992 ("gains accruing to an AUT [and OEIC] shall not be chargeable gains") is sufficient. There is no need for the further protection that section 468AA might provide.

21) But in the unlikely event that profits from contracts outside the scope of the charging provisions in the new schedule were ever accounted for as income, the expectation is that treatment would follow for tax. It is not justified to afford funds the blanket protection they have previously had from section 468AA in such circumstances. It would be inconsistent with the treatment of profits that are subject to the new Derivative Contracts Schedule.

Transitional Arrangements

What arrangements are there to provide for transition from the old rules to the new?

22) Transitional rules for derivative contracts are not necessary because AUTs and OEICs were not "qualifying companies" for the purposes of the financial instruments legislation.

23) But for loan relationships, a number of transitional rules relating to interest in general, the accrued income scheme and relevant discounted securities have been made to ensure that no amount is either taxed twice or relieved twice.

Offshore Fund Consequentials

Currently the UK Equivalent profits (UKEP) of a "distributing" offshore fund are calculated on the basis that the income tax rules relating to unauthorised unit trusts (UUTs) apply to the offshore fund's creditor loan relationships. This was in line with the previous treatment of AUTs and OEICs, so has there been any change?

24) No. UKEP will still be calculated on the existing UUT basis. The offshore funds regime is however under review. So, subject to the outcome of that review, there may be further change.

And is the position the same for an offshore fund's derivative contracts?

25) Yes. The UUT income tax rules will apply to the calculation of UKEP in respect of an offshore fund's derivative contracts as they will for its creditor loan relationships.

Contacts

Mike Howe
Tel: 020 7438 8421
E-mail: Mike.Howe@ir.gsi.gov.uk

Graham Turner
Tel: 020 7438 7517
E-mail: Graham.Turner@ir.gsi.gov.uk'

25.31   **Anti-avoidance: qualifying contracts with non-residents.** The following note is added after list (i)–(iii).

'As regards (i) above, for the guidelines used by the Revenue in deciding whether a company should be approved as a financial trader, see Revenue Pamphlet IR 131, SP 3/95, 21 March 1995 (now superseded by SP 4/02, 30 September 2002).'

25.32A   A new section is added as follows.

'**Anti-avoidance: currency contracts and currency options.** Legislation is to be introduced in the 2003 Finance Bill with retrospective effect for contracts entered into or varied **on or after 30 September 2002**. It applies where a qualifying company (see 25.17 above) becomes party to a qualifying contract which is a currency contract or currency option (see 25.18 above), or where the terms of such a contract held by such a company are varied, and the following conditions are, or subsequently become, satisfied:

(*a*)   in accordance with generally accepted accounting practice (see 51.1 PROFIT COMPUTATIONS), the company, in preparing its statutory accounts, uses the exchange rate implied by the contract (the "accounting rate"); and

(*b*)   there is a difference between the accounting rate and the "final payment rate" of more than 1% of the "final payment rate".

The "*final payment rate*" is the exchange rate found by reference only to amounts which fall, or would apart from these provisions fall, to be regarded for the purposes of *FA 1994, s 150(2)* or *(7)* (see 25.18 above), as the case may be, as the amounts of the currency to be received, and the currency to be paid in exchange, under the contract.

Where this provision first applies in relation to the contract in an accounting period beginning before 1 October 2002, the relevant derivative contracts rules (see 25.2 *et seq.* above) have effect in relation to the contract for that and any subsequent accounting period.

Similar provision is made in relation to a qualifying contract which is a currency contract which arises from the exercise of a currency option which is or was itself a qualifying contract (or a series of such options) and which (or any one of which) was entered into or varied on or after 30 September 2002.

For the draft legislation itself, see Revenue Internet Statement 30 September 2002.'

28   Friendly Societies

28.7   **Non-exempt life and endowment business.** It is noted that *SI 1997 No 473* is further amended by *SI 2003 No 23*.

29   Groups of Companies

29.2   **Intra-group dividends, charges and interest: companies resident in EU Member States.** A reference is added to the case of *Pirelli Cable Holding NV and Others v CIR Ch D, [2003] STC 250*, in which two UK companies paid dividends to two Italian companies in the same group. The effect of the double taxation agreement between the UK and Italy was that when the Italian companies received dividends from one of the UK companies, they received payments from the Revenue equal to 6.875% of the dividends. Following the decision in *Metalgesellschaft Ltd and Others v CIR CJEC (Case C-397/98), [2001] STC 452*, the UK companies claimed damages from the Revenue on the basis that the provisions of *ICTA 1988, s 247* contravened *Article 43EC* of the *EC Treaty*. The Ch D gave judgment for the companies. Park J held that the payments which the Revenue had made to the Italian companies in accordance with the double taxation agreement did not extinguish the fact that the UK subsidiaries had suffered cash-flow disadvantages as a result of the discriminatory provisions of *ICTA 1988, s 247*. Accordingly the UK subsidiaries were entitled to damages.

29.14   **Group relief.** A reference is added to the case of *Marks and Spencer plc v Halsey (Sp C 352), [2003] SSCD 70*, in which a UK company (M) established subsidiary companies in Belgium, France and Germany. These subsidiaries made losses. M claimed group relief on the basis that it should be entitled to set the losses which these companies made against its UK profits. The Revenue rejected the claim and M appealed, contending that the relevant provisions of the UK legislation, which prevented an EU-resident subsidiary trading outside the UK from surrendering losses to its ultimate UK parent, were a breach of *Article 43EC* of the *EC Treaty*. The Special Commissioners rejected this contention and dismissed the appeal, holding that 'the existence of different rules in the State of origin for taxing the foreign branch operations of its nationals or their foreign subsidiaries, thereby influencing its nationals' choice between the two forms of organisation, does not infringe *Article 43*'. The Commissioners also observed that 'the denial of UK relief for losses on activities the profits of which are not subject to UK tax can be justified as being for the maintenance of the coherence of the UK tax system'.

29.20   **Limits on group relief: relief for or in respect of non-resident companies.** A reference is added to an article in the Revenue Tax Bulletin (August 2002 p 961), reproduced below, concerning Revenue acquiescence in certain group relief claims.

'**GROUP RELIEF — ACCOUNTING PERIODS PRIOR TO 1 APRIL 2000 — UK BRANCHES OF COMPANIES RESIDENT IN THE EUROPEAN ECONOMIC AREA (EEA)**

We have recently considered a case involving group relief and UK branches of companies resident in another EU Member State.

The accounting periods concerned pre-date the introduction of the new group relief rules in Finance Act 2000. Claims had been made to surrender branch losses to a UK resident subsidiary of the EU resident parent and to set losses of UK resident subsidiaries against UK branch profits, and appeals had been made against decisions to refuse group relief. The basis of the appeals was that to deny group relief would be contrary to EC law.

We have decided not to contest those appeals, so the claims will now be accepted. We are advising Inspectors to settle any other similar cases, raising issues of group relief and UK branches of EEA resident companies prior to Finance Act 2000, on the same basis.

Finance Act 2000 introduced new rules governing group relief for branches. Those rules are in Section 403D and section 403E ICTA 1988 and apply in relation to accounting periods ending on or after 1 April 2000. There is an article about the new rules in Tax Bulletin 49 October 2000.'

31 Income Tax in relation to a Company

29.49 **Demergers: relief from tax on capital gains.** The second paragraph is revised as follows.

'For distributions before 17 April 2002, an exempt distribution within 29.36(*b*)(ii) above was regarded as a scheme of reconstruction for the purpose of relief under *TCGA 1992, s 139* (see 9.6 CAPITAL GAINS), so that the transfer of assets to the transferee company was, in relation to corporation tax on capital gains, treated as giving rise to neither gain nor loss. (Revenue Pamphlet IR 131, SP 5/85, 21 May 1985). See now 9.6 CAPITAL GAINS.'

29.57 **Demergers: clearance.** It is noted that applications for clearance should now be addressed to Mohini Sawhney, Fifth Floor, 22 Kingsway, London WC2B 6NR (or, if market-sensitive information is included, to Ray McCann at that address). Applications may be faxed to 020–7438 4409 or e-mailed to reconstructions@gtnet.gov.uk (after advising Ray McCann (on 020–7438 6585) if market-sensitive information is included). Application may now be made in a single letter to the same address for clearance under *ICTA 1988, s 215* and under any one or more of *ICTA 1988, s 225* (see 52.6 PURCHASE BY A COMPANY OF ITS OWN SHARES), *ICTA 1988, s 707* (transactions in securities, see Tolley's Income Tax under Anti-Avoidance), *TCGA 1992, s 138(1)* (share exchanges, see Tolley's Capital Gains Tax under Anti-Avoidance), *TCGA 1992, s 139(5)* (reconstructions involving the transfer of a business, see 9.6 CAPITAL GAINS), *TCGA 1992, s 140B* (transfer of a UK trade between EC Member States, see 9.8 CAPITAL GAINS), *TCGA 1992, s 140D* (transfer of non-UK trade between EC Member States, see 9.9 CAPITAL GAINS) and *FA 2002, Sch 29 para 88* (see 38.26 INTANGIBLE ASSETS).

31 Income Tax in relation to a Company

31.3 **Certain payments by companies and local authorities.** It is noted that from 1 December 2002, by virtue of *SI 2002 No 2931*, payments to nominees for the exempt bodies listed in (*c*)(i)–(xiii) may be made gross.

33 Inland Revenue: Administration

33.11 **Use of electronic communications.** The second paragraph is revised as follows.

'See *The Income and Corporation Taxes (Electronic Communications) Regulations 2003 (SI 2003 No 282)* (which replace the *Regulations 2000 (SI 2000 No 945)* as amended) and directions thereunder by the Commissioners, which make provision for electronic communications in relation to delivery of returns and other information under *TMA 1970, ss 8–9, 9A–9D, 12AA, 12AB, 12AC–12AE, 59DA, 59E* or *Sch 1A* or *FA 1998, ss 30–36* or *Sch 18* and payments or repayments in connection with the operation of those provisions. See also *SI 2002 No 680*.'

A reference is also added to an article in the Revenue Tax Bulletin (February 2003 pp 995, 996), reproduced below, summarising the mandatory e-filing requirements.

'**IMPORTANT CHANGES TO THE FILING OF EMPLOYER END OF YEAR RETURNS**

The Government believes that encouraging employers to make greater use of new technology is the best way to help them deal with their payroll tasks.

As part of the measures to support this change all employers will be required to file their End of Year returns electronically (e-) by 2010, either directly or through an intermediary, such as a payroll bureau or agent.

All employers with 250 or more employees will be required to e-file End of Year forms by May 2005.

Detail

The compulsory electronic filing date will depend on the number of employees an employer has:

Number of Employees	First compulsory electronic Return	Deadline
250 or more	2004/05 End of Year	May 2005
Between 50 and 249	2005/06 End of Year	May 2006
Fewer than 50	2009/10 End of Year	May 2010

The primary legislation for compulsory electronic filing is in sections 135 and 136 FA 2002. The draft regulations are expected to be published on the Inland Revenue website in March 2003. Copies may also be obtained from Press Office.

What is e-filing?

E-filing means employers will have to send their End of Year returns (both forms P35 and P14 together) by:

- Internet service for PAYE **or**

- Electronic Data Interchange (EDI) service **or**

- using an intermediary, such as a payroll bureau or agent, who will submit End of Year returns on the employers behalf using one of the above.

PLEASE NOTE: Magnetic media (CD ROM, flexible disk, data cartridge and open reel tape) are not considered electronic.

Penalties

There will be a new penalty of up to £3000 per annum per PAYE scheme for the employer's failure to make an electronic End of Year return when they should have done so. This is in addition to the existing late filing penalty.

Financial Incentives

There will be financial incentives for employers with fewer than 50 employees to encourage them to make the transition from paper to e-filing earlier. All qualifying employers who successfully e-file for these years will receive the payment shown in the table, including those who are already e-filing.

End of Year Return	2004/05	2005/06	2006/07	2007/08	2008/09
Incentive (£)	250	250	150	100	75

What now

- Most agents are employers, so will have to prepare to meet their own obligation to e-file as well as considering how they will help their employer clients with e-filing.

- Agents can also help their clients by letting them know that this change is coming.

- Agents should establish that they will meet the electronic submission requirements (as shown on previous page).

- Agents who want to e-file and are already using payroll software should contact their software provider to ascertain which of the 2 services it will support and from what date, and the range of electronic forms and returns it will support (eg forms P14, P35, P6, P9 etc).

47

- Agents who do not already have payroll software should start considering their options now. If they use an IT payroll product they should find it will help and enable them to deal more easily with their payroll obligations. When employers, intermediaries or agents decide to file electronically they need to consider:

- which service to use; and

- what software or hardware they need to buy. Employers and agents will need to make sure that the payroll software that they choose include an electronic submission capability.

Details of software which is formally accredited by IR can be found at: http://www.inlandrevenue.gov.uk/ebu/acclist.htm. The IR accreditation process checks that the payroll software accurately calculates tax, NICs, student loan deductions etc and also ensures that it incorporates one of the two electronic transmission service requirements.

Details of software which is EDI certificated can be found at: http://www.inlandrevenue.gov.uk/ebu/eb4_paye_edi.pdf

Details of software which has been IR checked as meeting the requirements of Internet transmissions can be found at: http://www.inlandrevenue.gov.uk/efiling/paye/paye_software_forms.htm.

Agents and Employers can find more information about EDI, the Internet service for PAYE and all the other services available on the Inland Revenue Website at: http://www.inlandrevenue.gov.uk/ebu/emp_index.htm

Additional information about the compulsory filing of employers End of Year returns, including financial incentives available, can be found on the Inland Revenue website at http://www.inlandrevenue.gov.uk/employers/ppip/index.htm'

34   Inland Revenue Explanatory Pamphlets etc.

The following new or substantially revised pamphlets are listed.

IR 1	Extra-Statutory Concessions as at 31 August 2002 (November 2002).
IR 2	Occupational Pension Schemes: A Guide for Members of Tax Approved Schemes (February 2003).
IR 5	Winding-Up Proceedings in England and Wales (October 2002).
IR 8	Winding-Up Petitions (November 2002).
IR 40 (CIS)	Construction Industry Scheme: Conditions for Getting a Sub-contractor's Tax Certificate (October 2002).
IR 68	Accrued Income Scheme (December 2002).
IR 116 (CIS)	A Guide for Subcontractors with Tax Certificates (February 2003).
IR 131	Statements of Practice as at 31 August 2002 (December 2002).
IR 137	The Enterprise Investment Scheme (January 2003).
IR 140	Non-resident Landlords, their Agents and Tenants (October 2002).
IR 160	Inland Revenue Enquiries under Self-Assessment (December 2002).

IR 169   Venture Capital Trusts — A Brief Guide (November 2002).

IR 176   Green Travel — A Guide for Employers and Employees on Tax and National Insurance Contributions (February 2003).

IR 179   R & D Tax Credits (August 2002).

IR 180   Construction Industry Scheme — A Guide for Non-residents (March 2003).
(CIS)

CGT 1   Capital Gains Tax — An Introduction (August 2002).

CWG 2   Employer's Further Guide to PAYE and NICs (April 2002).

AO 1   How to Complain about the Inland Revenue and the Valuation Office Agency (August 2001).

CWL 5   The Voluntary Arrangements Service (October 2002).

35   Inland Revenue Extra-Statutory Concessions

It is noted that a revised Revenue Pamphlet IR 1 (2002) has been published containing all current concessions as at 31 August 2002.

36   Inland Revenue Press Releases

The following additional press releases are listed.

17.4.02 **Taxation of UK branches of foreign companies.** Legislation is to be introduced in
(REV/BN 25) the 2003 Finance Bill substituting a 'permanent establishment' test for the branch or agency concept. See 54.4 RESIDENCE.

17.4.02 **Supporting small businesses and entrepreneurs.** The planned implementation of
(REV/C&E payroll electronic filing is set out. See 33.11 INLAND REVENUE: ADMINISTRATION.
2/02)

27.11.02 **A modern and competitive business tax system.** A number of changes are proposed
(REV & CE1) concerning corporation tax and employee share schemes. See 51.9 PROFIT COMPUTATIONS.

27.11.02 **Draft clause — application of CFC provisions to Hong Kong and Macao companies.** Special provision is to be made in the Finance Bill 2003 with full retrospective effect. See 18.14 CONTROLLED FOREIGN COMPANIES.

27.11.02 **Draft legislation — CFCs — extended warranties, credit protection and similar business.** Anti-avoidance provisions are to be introduced in the 2003 Finance Bill with effect for CFC accounting periods beginning on or after 27 November 2002. See 18.14(1)(*b*) CONTROLLED FOREIGN COMPANIES.

27.11.02 **Draft legislation — taxation of UK branches of foreign companies** (see Press Release 17.4.02 (REV/BN 25) above). See 54.4 RESIDENCE.

27.11.02 **Policy statement — recognised stock exchanges.** A new approach to the designation of recognised stock exchanges is announced. See generally 13.6 CLOSE COMPANIES.

23.12.02 **Making taxation of life insurance companies fairer.** A number of changes are proposed for the 2003 Finance Bill. See 42.1 LIFE INSURANCE COMPANIES.

37   Inland Revenue Statements of Practice

It is noted that a revised Revenue Pamphlet IR 131 (2002) has been published containing all current Statements of Practice as at 31 August 2002. Also, the following additional Statements of Practice are listed.

SP 2/02   **Exchange rate fluctuations.** Revenue practice is explained. (Replaces SP 1/87 above, but does not apply to companies within the charge to corporation tax.) See 23.3, 23.4 EXCHANGE GAINS AND LOSSES.

SP 4/02   **Definition of financial trader for the purposes of FA 2002, Sch 26 para 31.** The guidelines used by the Revenue in deciding whether a company should be approved as a financial trader are explained. (Replaces SP 3/95 above.) See 25.10, 25.31 FINANCIAL INSTRUMENTS AND DERIVATIVE CONTRACTS.

SP 5/02   **Exemptions for companies' gains on substantial shareholdings: sole or main benefit test: TCGA 1992, Sch 7AC para 5.** Revenue guidance is given on the application of the anti-avoidance rule. See 10.7 CAPITAL GAINS — SUBSTANTIAL SHAREHOLDINGS.

38   Intangible Assets

38.26   **Clearance.** The following note is added.

'Applications for clearance should be addressed to Mohini Sawhney, Fifth Floor, 22 Kingsway, London WC2B 6NR (or, if market-sensitive information is included, to Ray McCann at that address). Applications may be faxed to 020–7438 4409 or e-mailed to reconstructions@gtnet.gov.uk (after advising Ray McCann (on 020–7438 6585) if market-sensitive information is included). Application may be made in a single letter to the same address for clearance under *FA 2002, Sch 29 para 88* and under any one or more of *ICTA 1988, s 215* (demergers, see 29.57 GROUPS OF COMPANIES), *ICTA 1988, s 225* (see 52.6 PURCHASE BY A COMPANY OF ITS OWN SHARES), *ICTA 1988, s 707* (transactions in securities, see Tolley's Income Tax under Anti-Avoidance), *TCGA 1992, s 138(1)* (share exchanges, see Tolley's Capital Gains Tax under Anti-Avoidance), *TCGA 1992, s 139(5)* (reconstructions involving the transfer of a business, see 9.6 CAPITAL GAINS), *TCGA 1992, s 140B* (transfer of a UK trade between EC Member States, see 9.8 CAPITAL GAINS) and *TCGA 1992, s 140D* (transfer of non-UK trade between EC Member States, see 9.9 CAPITAL GAINS).'

38.34   **Supplementary provisions: finance leasing etc..** It is noted that the initial regulations have been published as *SI 2002 No 1967*.

39   Interest on Overpaid Tax

39.2(C)   **Example: instalment payment.** The figures are adjusted following the rate change referred to at 49.1 PAYMENT OF TAX.

40   Interest on Unpaid Tax

40.2(C)   **Example: instalment payment.** The figures are adjusted following the rate change referred to at 49.1 PAYMENT OF TAX.

41 Investment Companies

41.2 **Management expenses.** The list of exclusions from payments treated as management expenses is extended to include costs incurred on mergers or acquisitions (whether or not abortive), following *Camas plc v Atkinson (Sp C 341), 2002 STI 1545*, in which a company (C) incurred substantial expenditure in evaluating a projected acquisition of another company. It did not proceed with the acquisition, and claimed relief for the expenditure as management expenses. The Revenue rejected the claim, and C appealed. The Special Commissioners dismissed the appeal, observing that the costs of acquiring investments did not qualify as management expenses, since 'to allow such expenses would produce a result that is inconsistent with the statutory scheme for imposing the tax charge on the investment company's income'. The costs of an 'extensive restructuring project' were 'not expenses of managing the company's investment business'.

41.6 **Open-ended investment companies.** It is noted that the *Open-ended Investment Companies (Tax) Regulations 1997 (SI 1997 No 1154)* are further amended by *SI 2002 No 1973*.

42 Life Insurance Companies

42.1 **Introduction.** The following note is added.

'**Prospective future legislation.** Legislation is proposed for the 2003 Finance Bill in a number of areas relating to life insurance companies. The following are the main proposed changes. For the detailed proposals, see Revenue Press Release and Internet Statement 23 December 2002 and the draft legislation published on the Revenue website.

Chargeable gains and allowable losses. The following will apply from 23 December 2002.

(*a*) *Ring-fencing.* Allowable losses accruing to the company other than on the disposal of long-term insurance fund assets will not be deductible against the policy holders' share of chargeable gains accruing on disposal of assets of that fund. Similarly allowable losses accruing on the disposal of long-term insurance fund assets will not be deductible from gains accruing to the company from disposal of assets outside that fund.

(*b*) *Deemed intra-group transfers.* An election under *TCGA 1992, s 171A* (see 9.20 CAPITAL GAINS) may be made for a deemed intra-group disposal before the disposal of an asset outside the group, but the deemed disposal will be treated as an asset other than an asset of the company's long-term insurance fund (so that (*a*) above applies to restrict relief).

(*c*) *Box transfers.* Losses accruing to a company on the deemed disposal of assets as a result of a transfer between the different categories of asset in *ICTA 1988, s 440(4)* (see 42.15 below) are deductible only from gains in the period in which the asset is disposed of outside the group (or by the company if it is not a member of a group). Similar rules will apply to debits arising from deemed related transactions under *section 440* in assets representing loan relationships and in derivative contracts.

(*d*) *"Bed and breakfast".* There will be rules to discourage "bed and breakfasting" of assets standing at a loss.

Case I profits. Subject to certain exceptions, for periods of account beginning after 31 December 2002, payments charged to, or transfers made out of, the company's investment reserve are to be treated as additional investment return and thus included in the computation of profit (see 42.4 below).

Other transfer of business proposals. A number of changes to the rules applying where a company transfers its business will apply for periods of account beginning after 31 December 2002.

Overseas life insurance companies. Many of the above proposed changes will also be applied to overseas life insurance companies.

Friendly societies. Some of the above proposed changes will also affect friendly societies carrying on life or endowment business.'

42.16   **Transfers of long-term business: clearance applications.** It is noted that the address for clearance applications is now Robert Peel, Revenue Policy, Business Tax, Room 5W2, 5th Floor, 22 Kingsway, London WC2B 6NR (or, if one or more of the parties is a non-UK resident company or a friendly society, to Richard Thomas at that address).

44   Loan Relationships

44.3   **Charge to, and relief from, tax.** A final paragraph is added as follows.

'*Deficit brought forward from previous regime.* Legislation is to be introduced in the Finance Bill 2003, with retrospective effect, preventing any amount of non-trading deficit carried forward under *FA 1996, s 83(3)* from an accounting period beginning before 30 September 2002 to an accounting period beginning on or after that date from being set against anything other than non-trading profits. (Revenue Internet Statement 30 September 2002).'

44.5   **Computation of debits and credits: exchange gains and losses.** It is noted that the draft *Exchange Gains and Losses (Savings, Transitional Provisions and Consequential Amendments) Regulations 2002* and *Exchange Gains and Losses (Bringing into Account Gains or Losses) Regulations 2002* have now been published as, respectively, *SI 2002 No 1969* and *SI 2002 No 1970*.

44.8   **Loan relationships for unallowable purposes.** A reference is added to an article in the Revenue Tax Bulletin (February 2003 pp 1001, 1002), reproduced below, giving a specific application of the unallowable purposes rule.

'AVOIDANCE VIA EMPLOYEE REMUNERATION PACKAGES: LOANS IN TURKISH LIRA AND OTHER "SOFT" CURRENCIES

In recent years, we have seen a variety of schemes involving the payment of remuneration to employees in non-cash form designed primarily to avoid income tax and NICs. Specific legislation to counter several types of scheme has been enacted and indeed an announcement was made in the Pre Budget Report on 27 November 2002 that immediate legislation was to be introduced to counter the abuse of Employee Benefit Trusts.

One particular avoidance scheme has attracted considerable media attention recently. Under that scheme, instead of part of an employee's remuneration – for example, a bonus – being in cash, there is a loan to the employee in a soft currency such as the Turkish lira that is expected to depreciate substantially against sterling. The employee can expect to realise an exchange gain in sterling terms when the loan is repaid which represents his or her "bonus" while the employer makes an equivalent exchange loss.

The Revenue's view is that, for accounting periods beginning on or after 1 October 2002, the unallowable purpose provisions in Paragraph 13 Schedule 9 FA 1996 – which were extended in Finance Act 2002 to cover exchange gains and losses – will normally apply to deny relief for the exchange loss. For earlier accounting periods, we believe that the anti-avoidance provisions in Sections 135/136 FA 1993 apply to disallow the exchange loss.

The tax and NICs treatment of payments made in this way will depend upon the precise contractual arrangements between employer and employee. A detailed investigation of all the facts surrounding the payment will be required in every case to determine the precise contractual arrangements.'

Partnerships involving companies. The following paragraph is added.

'Where the company's accounting date or functional currency differs from that of the partnership, the Revenue consider that the company is not required to substitute its own accounting date or functional currency for that of the partnership in computing the company partner's credits and debits. (Revenue Tax Bulletin December 2002, pp 987–989).'

The Revenue Tax Bulletin article referred to is as follows.

'PARTNERSHIPS AND LOAN RELATIONSHIPS

FA 2002 inserted a new paragraph 19 into Schedule 9 FA 1996 to deal comprehensively with cases where a company is a member of a partnership and a money debt (which includes a loan relationship) is owed by or to the partnership. Each company partner computes separately loan relationship debits and credits arising on the money debt.

For this purpose paragraph 19(4) Schedule 9 deems that the money debt is owed by or to the company partner, and that everything done by the partnership in relation to the debt has been done by the company.

The company then computes the debits and credits ("the gross debits and credits") that arise from applying the loan relationships rules to this deemed situation. The company partner brings into account a proportion of these gross debits and credits, the proportion being determined by reference to the partner's interest in the partnership.

We have been asked whether paragraph 19(4) means that you effectively ignore the existence of the partnership. The question arises in two circumstances:

• the company partner and the partnership have different accounting dates, or

• the functional currency of the partnership differs from that of the company partner. For example, a company that prepares accounts in sterling may have an investment in a partnership that prepares financial statements in US dollars.

Our view is that paragraph 19(4) requires the company partner to imagine itself as "standing in the shoes" of the partnership. The company is not required to substitute its own accounting date, or its own functional currency, for that of the partnership.

Case law on deeming provisions shows that the application of a "statutory fiction" should be carried only so far as is necessary for the purposes of the statute. The purpose of the deeming exercise in paragraph 19(4) is to compute the debits or credits accruing to the company partner, in a way that takes account of the particular circumstances of that company. There is no need, in doing this, to pretend that the partnership does not exist at all.

Example 1 illustrates how a company partner's loan relationships debits and credits are calculated where its accounting date differs from that of the partnership. Example 2 illustrates the computation where the partnership has a different functional currency.

Example 1

X Ltd is a trading company with an accounting date of 31 December. It is a partner in a partnership P, which prepares accounts to 31 March. It does not account for its investment in P on a mark to market basis.

On 1 May 2003, the partnership acquires a zero coupon bond (issued by an unconnected company). The partnership accounts for the bond on an accruals basis. Its accounts show a credit of £50,000 in the year to 31 March 2004 in respect of accrued discount on the bond, and a similar credit of £80,000 in the year to 31 March 2005.

X Ltd is entitled to 50% of the profits of P in the year to 31 March 2004, but to only 25% in the year to 31 March 2005.

Step 1 — calculate gross credits

Under paragraph 19(4), the "gross credits" are computed as if the zero coupon bond were a creditor loan relationship to which X Ltd is a party for the purposes of its own trade. The company must account for this deemed loan relationship on an authorised accruals basis (paragraph 19(10)). X Ltd (and any other company partner) computes "gross credits" for periods of account ending on 31 March.

X Ltd therefore has gross trading loan relationship credits of £50,000 in the year to 31 March 2004, and £80,000 in the year to 31 March 2005.

The company is not required to work out the discount that would accrue on the bond in year ended 31 December 2003, or subsequent accounting periods.

Step 2 — compute the "appropriate share" of gross credits for each AP of X Ltd

Paragraph 19(6) says that apportionment of gross credits between partners is to be according to the shares that would be found by S114(2) ICTA88. Although paragraph 19(2) disapplies S114(1) ICTA88 where loan relationships are concerned, the apportionment rules in S114(2) continue to apply, including the provision for apportioning profits or losses to the corresponding accounting periods of the company.

X Ltd's apportioned credits are £25,000 (50% x £50,000) for the year to 31 March 2004, and £20,000 (25% x £80,000) for the year to 31 March 2005.

X Ltd will therefore need to time-apportion these sums between its own accounting periods, and bring in:

Year ended 31 December 2003: 275/366 x £25,000 = £18,784

Year ended 31 December 2004: (91/366 x £25,000) + (275/365 x £20,000) = £21,284

Example 2

Y plc is entitled to 40% of the profits of a partnership, Q. Y plc accounts in sterling; partnership Q accounts in dollars. Both Y plc and Q prepare accounts to 31 December. Y plc uses the closing rate/net investment method to translate its investment in the partnership, using an average exchange rate for the year to translate its share of Q's profit into sterling.

In the year to 31 December 2004, Q borrows $5 million from a bank. The bank is not connected with Y plc or any other company partner. Interest of $200,000 is payable on the loan during the period.

During the year the partnership sold goods to a customer for €10,000. The invoice remained unpaid at the year end. Q translated the trade debt into dollars at the year end, bringing into its accounts an exchange gain of $500.

Step 1 — calculate gross debits and credits

The gross debits and credits are calculated in the functional currency of the partnership. Paragraph 19(10) requires an authorised accruals basis to be used. Thus there is a debit of $200,000 in respect of the loan interest. S100(1) and (2) FA96 also requires exchange differences on the Euro trade debt (which is a money debt, but not a loan relationship) to be accounted for under the loan relationships rules. This gives rise to a gross credit of $500.

Step 2 — apportion gross debits and credits to the company partner

Since Y plc is entitled to 40% of partnership profits, it must bring into account a debit of $80,000 and a credit of $200 (or a net amount of $79,800). In accordance with S94AB(1) and (2) FA93, this is translated into sterling at the rate used in Y plc's accounts to translate the partnership profits. If the average rate used is, say, $1.6/£, Y plc would show a loan relationship debit of £49,875 (79,800 divided by 1.6) in its tax computations.

Similar principles apply where a partnership is a party to a derivative contract (paragraph 49 Sch 26 FA 2002).'

44.12 **Collective investment schemes: authorised unit trusts and open-ended investment companies.** The following note is added.

'For a statement agreed between the Revenue and the Investment Management Association confirming the tax treatment in these circumstances, see Revenue Tax Bulletin August 2002 pp 948–950.'

The Revenue Tax Bulletin article referred to is reproduced at 25.11 FINANCIAL INSTRUMENTS AND DERIVATIVE CONTRACTS.

44.14 **Transitional provisions: deferred foreign exchange gains.** It is noted that the draft *Exchange Gains and Losses (Savings, Transitional Provisions and Consequential Amendments) Regulations 2002* and *Exchange Gains and Losses (Bringing into Account Gains or Losses) Regulations 2002* have now been published as, respectively, *SI 2002 No 1969* and *SI 2002 No 1970*.

49 Payment of Tax

49.1 **Accounting periods ending after 30 September 1993: self-assessment: instalment payments.** It is noted that, with effect from 17 February 2003, the rates of interest on unpaid and overpaid instalments are reduced to 4.75% and 3.50% respectively.

49.9 **Certificates of tax deposit.** It is noted that the minimum initial deposit and addition are now £500 and £250 respectively.

51 Profit Computations

51.2 **Corporation tax computations.** The following paragraph is added.

'Under the Tax Law Rewrite programme, the provisions relating to income from employment, previously within Schedule E, are rewritten as part of the *Income Tax (Earnings and Pensions) Act 2003* ("*ITEPA 2003*"), which has effect for income tax purposes for 2003/04 and subsequent years and for corporation tax purposes for accounting periods ending after 5 April 2003. For accounting periods which straddle that date, the company may elect (by notice to the Revenue within two years of the end of the accounting period) for the provisions as they applied prior to the rewriting to continue in force for that period. Otherwise, the transitional provisions in *ITEPA 2003* apply to the straddling period as if references to the tax year 2003/04 were references to the straddling period and as if references to 6 April 2003 were to the first day of the straddling period. Certain provisions relating to employee share schemes do not have effect for any part of an accounting period which falls before 6 April 2003. [*ITEPA 2003, s 723, Sch 7 paras 90–92*].'

51 Profit Computations

51.9   **Employee share schemes.** Following *ICTA 1988, s 85B, Sch 4AA* (introduced by *ITEPA 2003*), the following is added at the end of the section relating to share incentive plans.

'*Contributions to plan trust.* With effect **from 6 April 2003**, a trading deduction is allowed for a payment made by a company to the trustees of a plan to enable them to acquire shares in the company or in a company which controls it, provided that:

(i)   the payment is so applied by the trustees;

(ii)   the shares are not acquired from a company; and

(iii)   twelve months after the date of the acquisition, the shares held by the trustees for the plan trust in the company whose shares are acquired constitute not less than 10% of the company's ordinary share capital and carry rights to not less than 10% of any profits available for distribution to shareholders and of any company assets available for distribution to shareholders in the event of a winding-up. Shares appropriated to, and acquired on behalf of, an individual under the plan are taken into account for this purpose until they cease to be subject to the plan.

The payment is allowed as a deduction in full for the period of account in which (iii) above is satisfied. No other deduction is allowed (except as below) for a payment so allowed, and no deduction may be made (as above) for the market value of shares when they are awarded.

The deduction may be *withdrawn* by Revenue notice where 30% of the shares acquired by the payment have not been awarded under the plan within five years of their acquisition, or where all the shares have not been so awarded within ten years of their acquisition. The amount of the deduction will then be treated as a trading receipt for the period of account in which the notice is given. Where, however, after the giving of such notice, all the shares acquired by the payment are awarded under the plan, a further deduction is allowed for the payment for the period of account in which the last of the shares is so awarded. No other deduction is allowed for a payment so allowed.

Where plan shares are awarded to an individual within (*a*) above (i.e. he is not a Schedule E taxpayer), a corresponding proportion of the deduction allowed under this provision is brought in as a trading receipt for the period of account in which the shares were so awarded. Similarly where a plan is terminated before all the shares in respect of which a deduction has been allowed under this provision have been awarded under the plan, a corresponding proportion of the deduction is brought in as a trading receipt for the period of account in which the plan termination notice is given.

For these purposes, shares acquired by the trustees on an earlier day are assumed to have been awarded to employees under the plan before those acquired on a later day.'

In consequence, the following is added to list (*a*)–(*d*).

'(*e*)   (from 6 April 2003) a deduction has been allowed for a contribution to the plan trust for acquisition of the shares (see below).'

Also, the following note is added.

'**Proposed future legislation.** The 2003 Finance Bill is to provide for a statutory corporation tax deduction for the cost of providing shares to employee share schemes where the employees are subject to UK tax on award of the shares (or would be but for their being obtained under a Revenue approved share scheme or Enterprise Management Incentive). This will apply to accounting periods beginning on or after 1 January 2003, and the relief referred to above for contributions to ESOP trusts will accordingly cease to apply to such periods. Certain deductions available under *FA 2000, Sch 8* (share incentive plans, see Tolley's Income Tax under Share Incentives and Options) take priority over deductions under the new provisions. See Revenue Press Release 27 November 2002 and the draft legislation and technical commentary published on the Revenue website on 19 December 2002. For an article on the interaction of the new provisions with the transfer pricing rules (see 4.4 ANTI-AVOIDANCE), see Revenue Tax Bulletin February 2003 pp 1002–1007.'

The Revenue Tax Bulletin article referred to is reproduced at 4.4 ANTI-AVOIDANCE.

51.20–
51.23
Research and development expenditure. Various references are added to a Special Edition of the Revenue Tax Bulletin (December 2002), reproduced below, giving a general description (with examples) of the three reliefs. In particular, 'staffing costs' and 'consumable stores' in 51.21(2) are clarified.

'RESEARCH AND DEVELOPMENT INCENTIVES

For many years tax relief has been given for virtually all the costs incurred by businesses on scientific research. Current expenditure received 100% relief under normal tax rules, and capital expenditure was given equivalent treatment in the form of "Scientific Research Allowances". These were renamed "Research and Development Allowances" in April 2000. At that time, some minor alterations were made to these allowances.

Also in April 2000, R&D tax credits were introduced for companies which are small or medium enterprises (SMEs). From 1 April 2000, SMEs can claim an extra tax deduction of 50% of their qualifying current R&D spending. Loss making SMEs can surrender their R&D losses in exchange for cash.

A further measure was introduced in April 2002, enabling "large" companies (non SMEs) to claim an extra deduction of 25% of qualifying current R&D spending.

A further relief, specifically targeted at research into drugs and medicines for TB, malaria and AIDS/ HIV – the so called "killer diseases" of the developing world – gives an additional 50% tax deduction (and repayments for loss making SME companies).

The detailed rules of the R&D tax credits for large companies and for SMEs are slightly different, although many of the basic definitions are the same. The essential difference is that the SME scheme is targeted at the company that commissions the work and takes the risks while the large company scheme is aimed at those companies that undertake the R&D.

This special edition of "Tax Bulletin" sets out the basic concepts of the R&D tax credits for both SMEs and large companies, and also those of the vaccines tax credit. Details of the long established R&D allowances are not covered.

For a full description of all aspects of the schemes, please see the Inland Revenue's guidance, available online at www.inlandrevenue.gov.uk/r&d

WHAT IS A SMALL OR MEDIUM SIZED COMPANY?

For the purposes of the three R&D reliefs we have incorporated into our legislation the European Commission definition of a small or medium sized enterprise. This is set out in Commission recommendation 96/280/EC of 3 April 1996.

A company is a **small or medium-sized enterprise (SME)** if it

• has fewer than 250 employees,

and

• has either

    • an annual turnover not exceeding €40 million, or

    • an annual balance sheet total not exceeding €27 million

and

• is independent of one or more large enterprises.

51   Profit Computations

An independent enterprise is one not more than 25% of whose capital or voting rights are owned by one enterprise or jointly by several enterprises which are not SMEs.

For example, a company 40% of whose capital is owned jointly by large companies is not an independent enterprise.

Holdings by venture capital companies, institutional investors and public investment corporations are ignored, unless they exercise control over the company. Where there is a change in the status of a company due to a change in the financial limits or the number of employees there is a year of grace before this takes effect.

Example

Mosler Ltd draws accounts up to 30 June each year. In the year 20 June 2003 it has 235 employees and this is increased to 260 in the following year and 265 in the year to June 2005. It fails the SME tests in the year to June 2004 but is held to be an SME in that year and only becomes a large company in the year to June 2005.

A large company is a company that does not qualify as a small or medium-sized enterprise.

THE THREE RELIEFS

1. R&D Tax relief for large companies

R&D tax relief for large companies is available for qualifying R&D expenditure incurred on or after 1 April 2002. (Schedule 12 Finance Act 2002.) The relief is given as an extra deduction — the scheme allows a large company to deduct an extra 25% of its revenue spending on R&D when it calculates its taxable profits. Capital spending on R&D does not qualify — it qualifies instead for 100% research and development allowances.

Relief is due where a company spends more than £25,000 on qualifying R&D expenditure in a 12 month accounting period. The £25,000 is adjusted proportionately if the accounting period is not 12 months long.

Example

Green Industries Plc is a large company. In its 12 month accounting period ended 30 April 2003 it has income of £30 million and expenses of £20 million including R&D spending of £4 million. Its accounts show a trading profit of £10 million (income £30 million less expenses £20 million). Its taxable profits, if there are no other adjustments for tax purposes, are £9 million (profits per accounts £10 million less R&D tax relief £1 million [= 25% x £4 million]).

Where one company subcontracts work to another, the relief goes to the company that does the work rather than the company that pays for the work to be done.

Although the scheme is aimed at large companies, a small or medium sized (SME) company can obtain the relief (at the large company rate) if it does R&D as a sub-contractor to a non-SME. Usually, this would be a large company, but it could include, for example, a Government department or a university.

Conditions to be satisfied

Expenditure must be incurred on or after 1 April 2002.

Pre-trading expenditure is normally treated as incurred on the day that trading begins (Section 401 ICTA88). This rule is overridden for the R&D relief for accounting periods straddling April 2002 — it is the date on which the pre-trading expenditure is actually incurred rather than the date on which it is treated as incurred that matters.

R&D tax relief for an accounting period is based on the qualifying R&D expenditure for that accounting period. Expenditure is qualifying R&D expenditure for an accounting period if it is deducted in computing trading profits for that period.

In certain circumstances a company may choose to defer the expenditure on R&D and not set it against the profits of that period. Where a company treats R&D expenditure in this way by including it to the balance sheet when it is incurred, that expenditure does not qualify for R&D tax relief when it is spent but when it is included it as a deduction in the profit and loss account (provided all the other conditions are satisfied in the period it is released).

Expenditure that can be deducted once the company starts trading is included in the qualifying R&D expenditure for the first period of trading provided that it is incurred on or after 1 April 2002.

The qualifying R&D expenditure for a 12 month accounting period must be at least £25,000 for R&D tax relief to be due. If the accounting period is some other length the £25,000 is adjusted proportionately. For example, if the accounting period is 8 months long, the qualifying R&D expenditure must be at least £16,667 (= £25,000 x 8/12).

Where an accounting period straddles 1 April 2002, it is split into two separate accounting periods and the £25,000 limit applies to the period that begins 1 April 2002.

Example

Alchemists Plc is a large company. It has an accounting date of 30 June. In the year ended 30 June 2002 it spends £60,000 on consumable stores for its research at a rate of £5,000 a month. It cannot claim R&D tax relief for the year ended 30 June 2002 even though it has spent more than £25,000 on R&D in that year. It has only spent £15,000 on consumable stores in the three month period that begins 1 April 2002.

Qualifying R&D expenditure

For a large company there are three types of qualifying R&D expenditure —

•   expenditure on direct research and development

•   expenditure on research and development sub-contracted to certain organisations

•   contributions to certain independent research and development organisations.

Qualifying expenditure on direct research and development is expenditure a company incurs on R&D work either for itself or, as a sub-contractor, for some other person. In either case, the company carries out the work itself: it does not pay someone else to do it.

The expenditure must satisfy all of these conditions;

•   It is incurred on research and development (see [below]) directly undertaken by the company.

•   It is incurred on staffing costs or consumable stores (see [below]).

•   It is attributable to relevant research and development (see [below]) in relation to the company.

•   It is not capital expenditure.

Where a company incurs expenditure carrying out activities contracted out to it, the expenditure does not qualify for R&D tax relief unless the contracting out was done by

•   a large company,

or

•   a person not in the course of a trade, profession or vocation assessable under Case I or II of Schedule D.

This means that a large company may claim relief for research carried out by it on behalf of another large company, a charity, a government agency or a company resident overseas —

but not for research carried out on behalf of an SME (unless it is a foreign SME), because the SME itself will be covered by the R&D tax relief scheme for SMEs.

Example

Green Enterprises Plc is a large company. The government of Freedonia contracts Green Enterprises Plc. to do some R&D for it. Green Enterprises spends £2.4 million doing that research in its accounting year ended 30 April 2004. Green Enterprises can claim an extra deduction of £600,000 (= 25% x £2.4 million) when it calculates its taxable profits for the year ended 30 April 2004.

Green Enterprises Plc would also be able to claim R&D tax relief if the R&D was contracted out to it by another large company or a charity or a UK government agency.

Qualifying expenditure on research and development sub-contracted to certain organisations

On occasions, companies may sub-contract part or all of their R&D to individuals or to organisations that cannot themselves benefit from the R&D tax relief. To accommodate such situations the legislation allows the contracting large company to claim relief on payments to certain persons and organisations who cannot benefit from R&D tax relief in their own right (but not, in general, when the work is sub-contracted to another company which could itself benefit).

The R&D must be carried out by an individual, a partnership of individuals, or a qualifying body (see [below]). These persons and organisations do not have to be resident in the UK.

Such expenditure must satisfy the following conditions:

•   The sub-contracted R&D must be directly undertaken on behalf of the company

•   the expenditure must be attributable to relevant research and development (see page 14) in relation to the company

and

•   the expenditure must not be capital.

"Directly undertaken on behalf of a company" means that the sub-contractor should do the work itself, not subcontract it in turn to another party.

Example

Green Enterprises Plc. wants to have some research done into new materials but instead of doing it itself it makes a contract with Necessity Inc., a company resident in the USA, to do the research for it for £3 million. It cannot claim R&D tax relief on the £3 million it pays to Necessity Inc. because Necessity Inc. is not an individual, a partnership of individuals or a qualifying body.

Green Enterprises Plc could claim R&D tax relief if it paid the £3 million to a university, a scientific research organisation, an individual or a partnership of individuals, none of which can claim R&D tax relief, to do the research for it.

Contributions to independent research and development qualify for R&D tax relief if they are made to a qualifying body, an individual or partnership of individuals. The R&D towards which the contribution is made must be relevant research in relation to the company making the contribution.

The sort of contributions this covers are payments which fall outside a contractual framework. However, the R&D must still be relevant R & D for the company that makes the payment.

Example

Green Enterprises Plc. hears on the grapevine that the University of Middle Earth is pursuing a line of research that is relevant research for Green Enterprises Plc and so it makes a payment of £5 million to the university department that is carrying out the research. Green Enterprises Plc. can claim R&D tax relief on that payment.

Such contributions do not qualify for R&D tax relief if

●   the funded research and development is contracted out to the qualifying body etc by someone else

●   the company is connected with an individual or any member of a partnership to whom the contribution is made.

Insurance companies

There are special rules for insurance companies.

An insurance company that carries on a life assurance business and qualifies as an SME is treated as a large company for the purposes of R&D tax relief. This means that it gets R&D tax relief at the large company rate (and subject to the rules applying specifically to SMEs) rather than the SME rate.

Group companies

Groups of companies may divide R&D work around the group, depending on where particular expertise resides or where facilities are available. When this happens, work undertaken by one of the companies may fall outside the definition of R&D because, seen only in the narrow context of the company undertaking the work, it is of a routine nature. For example, one group company may carry out testing procedures for all the other companies in the group. For the a company doing this, the testing in itself is not R&D but if it were done by the company that had carried out the basic R&D it may be.

When the contractor company and sub-contractor company are members of the same group, the activities of the contractor and sub-contractor are taken together in deciding whether the activities of the sub-contractor company are relevant R &D.

This means that if the sub-contractor company's activities would have amounted to R&D if the contractor company had carried them out itself, the sub-contractor company's activities are relevant R&D for it and it can claim R&D tax relief.

This only applies where R&D is contracted by another group company. It does not apply to activities contracted out to unconnected companies.

Refunds of payments or contributions

A company that has sub-contracted R&D or made a contribution to independent R&D may receive a refund of its payment to the sub-contractor or its contribution. When that happens, an additional 25% of the refund is treated as Case 1 Schedule D income of the accounting period in which the refund is made.

2. R & D tax relief for small or medium sized companies (SMEs)

Outline

R&D tax credits for small or medium sized companies (SMEs) were introduced in 2000 (Schedule 20 Finance Act 2000.) R&D tax relief for SMEs is available for qualifying R&D expenditure (see page 6) incurred on or after 1 April 2000. Only companies may claim.

Relief is not due unless a company spends more than £25,000 on qualifying R&D expenditure in a 12 month accounting period. Non qualifying expenditure such as the purchase of capital assets is ignored when calculating whether the £25,000 limit has been reached.

The £25,000 is adjusted proportionately if the accounting period is not 12 months long. For example, if the accounting period is 10 months long the limit is £20,491 = £25,000 x 10/12.

If an accounting period straddles 1 April 2000 it is split and the periods before 1 April 2000 and from 1 April 2000 onwards are considered separately.

R&D tax relief allows an SME to deduct an extra 50% of its qualifying current spending on R&D when it calculates its taxable profits. If a SME has a "surrenderable loss" for an accounting period for which it is entitled to R&D tax relief it may surrender the loss arising from the R&D to the Exchequer in return for a payment. This (and nothing else), strictly, is the "R&D tax credit", although the term has passed into more general use to describe both the relief in general and the similar relief for large companies - which does not have a payable element.

Only revenue expenditure qualifies. As for large companies, capital expenditure on R&D qualifies for 100% research and development (capital) allowances.

R&D tax relief is not due unless any intellectual property created as a result of the R&D is vested at least in part in the SME that carried it out.

Normally, if a SME contracts out R&D to another person it is the SME that contracts out the work that may claim R&D tax relief rather than the person who does the R&D. This is unlike R&D tax relief for large companies, where in general it is the company that does the R&D that may claim the additional relief rather than the company that contracts it out.

There are a few exceptional cases where a SME may claim R&D tax relief for work that it does as a sub-contractor. A SME may claim R&D tax relief for work contracted out to it if the contracting out is done by a large company or a charity, a government agency or a person resident overseas outside the UK tax net. However, when this happens the SME claims under the terms of the "large company" R&D tax relief rather than the SME scheme.

If an SME makes claims under both schemes, its expenditure on its own behalf (for which it will claim under the SME scheme) and as a subcontractor (for which it will claim under the large company scheme) is aggregated for the purposes of the £25,000 yearly minimum in both schemes.

Summary of differences between large company and SME schemes

The rate of the extra R&D tax deduction in the large company scheme is 25% while the rate in the SME scheme is 50%.

In the SME scheme a company can claim relief for payments that it makes to subcontractors but in the large company scheme the relief normally goes to the company that carries out work as a sub-contractor.

The exception is that a large company may claim relief for subcontract payments made to persons who cannot benefit from the relief themselves, such as universities, charities, and individuals.

In the large company scheme there is no requirement that any intellectual property rights arising from the research are vested in the company claiming the R&D tax relief.

In the large company scheme subsidies received are not deducted from qualifying R&D expenditure.

Qualifying R&D expenditure

More precisely qualifying R&D expenditure of an SME company is expenditure that satisfies all of these conditions.

- It is not capital expenditure.
- It is attributable to relevant research and development (see [below]).
- It is incurred on staffing costs (see [below]) or consumable stores (see [below]).

- Any intellectual property created as a result of the R&D to which the expenditure is attributable is vested in the company.

- The company does not incur the expenditure as a sub-contractor.

- The expenditure is not subsidised.

- The expenditure is incurred on or after 1 April 2000.

Pre-trading expenditure is normally treated as incurred on the day that trading begins (Section 401 ICTA88). This rule is overridden for the R&D relief for accounting periods straddling April 2000 — it is the date on which the pre-trading expenditure is actually incurred rather than the date on which it is treated as incurred that matters.

Subsidised Expenditure

R&D tax relief is not available for the part of any expenditure in respect of which a grant or subsidy (other than a notified State aid) is obtained.

Example

Southside Ltd is an SME. It receives a grant towards the cost of a new laboratory. R&D tax relief is available in full on its qualifying costs because the grant was not towards an R&D project. The grant will be taken into account if the company wants to make a RDA claim on the capital costs of the laboratory.

If, however, Southside Ltd. receives a grant that covers 50% of the cost of an R&D project, that grant will be taken into account when R&D tax relief (and credit) is calculated. Only 50% of the spending on staffing costs and consumable stores will be taken into account in calculating the tax relief due, because the other 50% was subsidised.

Where a project has received funding which is a notified State aid (see page 15) then no expenditure on that project can qualify for the R&D SME relief, which is itself a notified state aid. Notified state aids are usually government funded grants such as the SMART award, but not all government grants are notified State aids — for example, some funding under the SMART label is not notified State aid (e.g. grants for feasibility studies and microenterprise awards).

If clarification of the status of a grant is needed, the body that has provided or arranged the funds should be able to help.

Intellectual Property (IP)

Any intellectual property created as a result of the R&D to which expenditure is attributable must be vested in the company for R&D tax credit to be available.

Intellectual property means

- know-how,

- a patent, trade mark, registered design, copyright, design right or plant breeder's right,

or

- any foreign rights similar to those above.

The IP does not have to be vested for a specified period of time and it may be held jointly with others. We also recognise that not all R&D activity results in any IP.

Sub-contracted R&D

A SME (the principal) may claim relief for payments to another person (the sub-contractor) for relevant R&D that it contracts out to that other person. The treatment varies depending on whether the two parties are connected or not.

51   Profit Computations

Principal and sub-contractor connected

For the principal to claim the relief in the accounting period that payment is made, the sub-contractor must include

- the payment

and

- its expenses incurred in carrying out the sub-contracted work

in its accounts for a period ending not more than 12 months after the end of the principal's accounting period in which it makes the payment.

The principal can claim the relief on the lower of:

- the payment that it makes to the sub-contractor, and

- the amount that the sub-contractor actually spends on staffing costs and consumable stores when it carries out the work for the principal in its accounting periods ending not more than 12 months after the end of the principal's accounting period in which the payment was made.

Example

As in the example above, Southside Ltd. is an SME. It contracts with Heliotrope Ltd., an SME with which it is connected, for Heliotrope to do research into the design and construction of mobile solar powered watchtowers. In its accounts year ended 24 May 2003 it pays Heliotrope Ltd. £4 million for the R&D.

Heliotrope Ltd. spends £3.5 million on staffing costs and consumable stores for the research it is doing for Southside Ltd in its accounts year ended 31 December 2003. It spends a further £1 million in its accounts year ended 31 December 2004.

Southside Ltd. may claim R&D tax credit of £3.5 million, because that is the lower of the amount it pays Heliotrope Ltd., £4 million, and the amount that Heliotrope Ltd. spends on the R&D in its accounts year ended 31 December 2003. The £1 million that Heliotrope Ltd. spends in the year ended 31 December 2004 is ignored because that accounting period ends more than 12 months after 24 May 2003, the end of Southside Ltd.'s accounting period in which it made the payment.

Principal and sub-contractor not connected

The principal may claim R&D tax relief on 65% of the payment it makes to the sub-contractor. This reflects the fact that the payment will cover an element of profit for the sub-contractor and also any other non qualifying expenditure that may be incurred.

If the principal and sub-contractor are not connected they may make a joint election to be treated as if they are connected. The election must be made by notice in writing given to an officer of the Board within 2 years of the end of the principal's accounting period in which the payment is made.

Example

If in the example above Southside Ltd. and Heliotrope Ltd. are not connected and do not make an election for connected persons treatment Southside Ltd may claim R&D tax credit of £2.6 million (= 65% x £4 million).

Work sub-contracted to a SME

Under the SME scheme, a SME may not claim R&D tax relief for work it does as a sub-contractor but in some cases it may claim under the large company scheme — see [above].

Relief given as a deduction

A SME company that

•   is carrying on a trade,

•   is entitled to R&D tax relief,

and

•   has qualifying R&D expenditure (see [above]) that is allowable as a deduction for an accounting period

may deduct 150% of that qualifying R&D expenditure when it computes its profits or losses.

This means that when it computes its profits for tax purposes it may deduct an extra 50% of its qualifying expenditure on R&D.

> *Example*
>
> Abelard Ltd. is an SME. It draws up its accounts to 30 June each year. In the year ended 30 June 2001 its accounts show a trading profit of £1.5 million. In arriving at those profits it deducted R&D expenditure of £2 million. If it makes a claim for R&D tax credit it may deduct an extra £1 million (150% x £2 million = £3 million – £2 million already deducted) when it computes its taxable profits. Its taxable profits, if there are no other adjustments for tax purposes, are therefore £500,000 (Profit per accounts £1.5 million less extra deduction for R&D tax credit £1 million).

Pre-trading expenditure

A company may incur expenditure on R&D before it starts to trade.

Normally pre-trading expenditure is treated by S 401 ICTA88 as incurred on the day that trading begins and so there is no relief for it until trading starts. R&D pre-trading expenditure for SMEs is an exception to this.

If a company incurs qualifying R&D expenditure in an accounting period in which it is not trading the company may make an election to treat 150% of that qualifying R&D expenditure as a trading loss for that accounting period.

The company can set this trading loss against any other profits it may have for that accounting period under S 393A(1)(a) ICTA88. For example, the company may receive interest in that accounting period. If it does, it can set the loss against that.

The company can carry the loss back and set it against its profits for the previous 12 months under S 393A(1)(b) ICTA88 provided that it was entitled to pre-trading R&D tax credit for that earlier accounting period.

The company can also surrender the loss as group relief or cash it in for the payable R&D tax credit.

Any unused losses are carried forward until the company starts to carry on a trade derived from the R&D. They are then treated as losses brought forward under S 393 ICTA88.

The election to treat 150% of the qualifying pre-trading R&D expenditure as a trading loss for an accounting period must be made by notice in writing to an officer of the Board within 2 years of the end of the accounting period to which it relates.

The company will not have accounting periods if it has not started to trade. It is treated as having the accounting periods it would have had if it had started to trade when it started the R&D activities.

If an election is made it applies to all of the company's qualifying R&D expenditure. The company cannot make a claim for part of its qualifying R&D expenditure.

51 Profit Computations

If the company claims to treat its qualifying pre-trading expenditure as a loss the expenditure is not treated as incurred on the first day of trading under S 401 ICTA88.

Example

Perception Ltd. is an SME. It has investment income of £1 million a year. It starts to carry out R&D on 1 April 2001 although it is not trading. It incurs expenditure on staffing costs and consumable stores at the rate of £30,000 a month. It starts to carry on a trade derived from the R&D on 1 October 2002.

The company makes an election to treat the pre-trading expenditure on R&D as a trading loss. It is treated as having a 12 month accounting period ended 31 March 2002 and so it must make the election for that period by 31 March 2004. It is also treated as having a 6 month accounting period from 1 April 2002 to 30 September 2002.

The R&D qualifying expenditure for the accounting period ended 31 March 2002 is £360,000 (= 12 months @ £30,000 a month). Perception Ltd.'s trading loss for that accounting period is £540,000 (= 150% x £360,000) and it can set that loss against its investment income of £1 million.

Payable R&D tax credits

A payable R&D tax credit allows an SME to claim payment from the Inland Revenue.

The basic rule is that an SME may claim a payable R&D tax credit for an accounting period in which it has a "surrenderable loss".

The surrenderable loss for an accounting period is the lower of

• 150% of the qualifying R&D expenditure for that accounting period,

and

• the unrelieved trading loss for that accounting period.

The unrelieved trading loss for an accounting period is the trading loss for that accounting period less

• any claim made, or that could have been made, under S 393A(1)(a) ICTA88 to set the loss against other profits of the period,

• any other relief given in respect of the loss; this includes losses set against profits of earlier periods under S 393(1)(b) ICTA88, and

• any loss surrendered under S403 ICTA88 as group or consortium relief.

Any losses brought forward from earlier accounting periods or carried back from later accounting periods are ignored.

Example

In its accounts year ended 24 May 2003, Southside Ltd. has qualifying R&D expenditure of £4 million and it makes a trading loss of £5 million. It surrenders losses of £2 million as group relief so that its unrelieved trading loss is £3 million (£5 million – £2 million surrendered as group relief). Its surrenderable loss for that accounting period is £3 million because that is the lower of its R&D relief £6 million (£4 million x 150%), and its unrelieved trading loss, £3 million.

If a company claims R&D tax credit the Inland Revenue pays it an amount in respect of the credit unless

• the company has outstanding Corporation Tax (CT) liabilities,

- there is an enquiry into the company's return for the accounting period for which the R&D tax credit is claimed

or

- there are outstanding PAYE and/ or Class 1 NICs for payment periods ending that accounting period.

If there are **outstanding Corporation Tax liabilities** the R&D tax credit may be used to discharge them. If that happens the R&D tax credit is treated as paid to the extent that it is so used.

If there is an **enquiry** into the company's return the Inland Revenue may withhold payment until the enquiry is completed: provisional payments may be made before the enquiry is completed.

If there are outstanding amounts of PAYE and/or Class 1 National Insurance it may be possible to offset the payable credit against such liabilities.

The amount of payable R&D tax credit to which a company is entitled for an accounting period is 16% of the surrenderable loss for that period.

There is a limit to this. The R&D tax credit payable to a company for an accounting period may not be more than the company's PAYE and NIC liabilities for payment periods ending in that accounting period in respect of all employees. A payment period is a period that ends on the 5th of the month and for which the company is liable to account for income tax and NIC to the Inland Revenue.

Where the company is a member of a group it is only the PAYE and NIC liabilities of the company making the claim that are taken into account.

The total of the company's PAYE and NIC liabilities for a payment period is the total of

- The gross amount of income tax for which the company is required to account to the Inland Revenue for that period, ignoring any deductions the company is authorised to make for working families' tax credit and disabled person's tax credit

- The gross Class 1 NICs paid for that payment period, ignoring any deductions the company is authorised to make for statutory sick pay, statutory maternity pay, working families' tax credit or disabled person's tax credit.

A payment of R&D tax credit is not income of the company. The company does not have to pay tax on it.

Example

Southside Ltd. claims R&D tax credit for its accounting period ended 24 May 2003. It has no outstanding CT liabilities and its PAYE and NIC payments are up to date. Its PAYE and NIC liabilities for that accounting period are £450,000. The company is paid £450,000, because that is the lower of £480,000, 16% of its surrenderable loss of £3 million for that accounting period, and £450,000, its PAYE and NIC liabilities. Thus only £2,812,500 of the relief is used leaving £187,500 to be carried forward.

Restriction of consortium relief

A company entitled to R&D tax relief may be owned by a consortium. In such a case if at least one of the consortium members is not a SME the company cannot surrender any losses as group relief to fellow consortium members that are not SMEs.

3. Vaccines research relief

Outline

Vaccines research relief (VRR) was introduced by Finance Act 2002 (Schedules 13 and 14). However, at the date of writing (November 2002) it had not been approved by the European

51   Profit Computations

Commission as a State aid and therefore was not in force. If and when it is approved the Inland Revenue will announce the date that it comes into force, which will be specified in a Treasury Order. (For the purposes of the examples in this section, it is assumed that the relief was in force at the time expenditure was incurred, unless otherwise stated.)

VRR gives companies additional relief for spending on research and development (R&D) (see [below]) into vaccines and medicines for the prevention and treatment of certain diseases. It is only available to companies. Individuals and partnerships of individuals cannot claim it.

The relief allows companies to deduct an additional 50 per cent of qualifying current R&D expenditure when they calculate their profits for corporation tax.

The relief will apply to expenditure incurred on or after the date specified by the Treasury Order. In determining whether expenditure was incurred after this appointed day, the rule in S 401 ICTA88 (which treats pre-trading expenditure as incurred on the day the trade begins) is ignored. It is the date on which the expenditure was actually incurred and not the date on which it is treated as incurred that matters.

The treatments and diseases covered are:

- vaccines and medicines for the prevention and treatment of tuberculosis and malaria,

- vaccines for the prevention of infection by human immunodeficiency virus ["HIV"], and

- vaccines and medicines for the prevention of the onset of, and the treatment of, acquired immune deficiency syndrome ["AIDS"] arising from particular strains of HIV found mostly in countries on the developing world.

Research must be into the diseases in humans. Other treatments do not qualify for VRR. For example, research into a vaccine to prevent bovine TB would not qualify for VRR.

VRR is not due unless a company spends more than £25,000 on qualifying expenditure on vaccines research in a 12 month accounting period. The £25,000 is adjusted proportionately if the accounting period is not 12 months long. For example, if a company has an accounting period that is 8 months long it must spend at least £16,777 (= £25,000 x 8/12) in that accounting period to qualify for VRR.

A company may incur expenditure that qualifies for both VRR and

- R&D tax relief for SMEs

or

- R&D tax relief for large companies.

Example

Festival Pharmaceuticals is a large company. It has £4 million of qualifying expenditure on research into a treatment for malaria in its accounts for the year ended 30 June 2005. In addition to its normal deduction of £4 million from income, it can deduct a further £1 million (= 25% x £4 million) large company R&D relief, since this work is R&D, and £2 million vaccines research relief (= 50% x £4 million) giving a total deduction of £7 million.

Companies can claim VRR for subcontract payments made to universities, charities and scientific research organisations, or for contributions to independent research carried on by such bodies.

Companies may also sub-contract research to other companies. When this happens VRR goes to the company that sub-contracts the research rather than the company that carries it out (regardless of the size of the companies concerned). So a company can claim VRR on sub-contract payments it makes to other companies. SMEs not in profit can surrender any losses arising from VRR in return for a payment of a vaccines tax credit (VTC) equal to 16% of the "surrenderable loss" arising from the VRR (calculated in a similar fashion to that for the general SME R&D scheme).

Example

Inventions Unlimited Ltd. is an SME. It spends £3 million on research into anti-HIV vaccines in its accounts year ended 31 May 2004. Those accounts show a loss of £5 million. It can claim

- VTC of £240,000 (= 16% x 50% x 3m)

and

- SME R&D tax credit of £720,000 (= 16% x 150% x 3m)

giving a total of £960,000.

Qualifying expenditure

There are three types of qualifying expenditure — qualifying expenditure on

- direct R&D,
- sub-contracted R&D, and
- contributions to independent R&D.

VRR is based on the qualifying expenditure for an accounting period.

There are different definitions of qualifying expenditure on direct or sub-contracted R&D for an accounting period for SMEs and large companies.

This means that SMEs can claim VRR on pre-trading expenditure when it is incurred but large companies have to wait until the trade begins.

Qualifying expenditure on direct R&D is expenditure incurred by a company on staffing costs (see [below]) or consumable stores (see [below]) for a qualifying R&D activity directly undertaken by the company and that satisfies the following conditions.

- The qualifying R&D activity must be relevant R&D (see [below]) in relation to the company.
- The expenditure must not be capital expenditure and it must not be subsidised (see [above]).
- The company must not incur the expenditure in carrying out activities contracted out to it by somebody else.

A qualifying R&D activity is R&D relating to certain specified diseases (see [below]).

A company can claim VRR for its qualifying expenditure on R&D which it has sub-contracted to someone else.

Qualifying expenditure on sub-contracted R&D is payments made by a company (the principal) for R&D contracted out by it to another person (the sub-contractor) that satisfy these conditions. There are two situations — either the sub-contractor is, or is not, a charity, university or scientific research organisation

(a) Where the sub-contractor is a charity, university or scientific research organisation

- The expenditure must not be subsidised (see [above]) or be capital expenditure.

- The expenditure must be on R&D directly undertaken by the sub-contractor on behalf of the company and must be on qualifying R&D activity.

- The R&D activity in respect of which the expenditure is incurred must be relevant R&D (see [below]) in relation to the company.

These are the only conditions that have to be satisfied.

(b) Where the sub-contractor is not a charity, university or scientific research organisation

The above conditions also have to be satisfied but there are further rules. These are the same as apply in the SME R&D scheme (see [above])

Sometimes a company can claim VRR on **contributions that it makes to independent R&D**. Relief is due if payments are made to

- a charity,

- a university, or

- a scientific research association

to fund qualifying R&D activity that the body carries on provided that the R&D is related to a trade carried on by the company that made the payments. Expenditure on contributions to independent R&D is qualifying expenditure for an accounting period if it is incurred in that accounting period.

Example

A company that manufactures vaccines may give a contribution to a charity that is carrying out research into a new AIDS vaccine. If it does that the company may claim VRR on the contribution.

We use the definitions of "charity" from S 506(1) ICTA88 and of "scientific research association" in S508 ICTA88. The effect of these is to restrict charities & SROs to bodies located in the UK. There is no similar restriction in the case of universities.

How VRR is given: SMEs

The general rule is that when an SME that is carrying on a trade is entitled to VRR for an accounting period the company may claim an additional deduction equal to 50% of the qualifying expenditure for that accounting period.

In the exceptional case where the qualifying expenditure does not qualify for R&D tax credits for SMEs the company may claim a deduction equal to 150% of the qualifying expenditure for the accounting period.

Pre-trading expenditure

If a SME company is entitled to VRR for pre-trading qualifying expenditure for an accounting period it may elect to be treated as if that pre-trading expenditure is a trading loss it had incurred in that accounting period. The election must specify the accounting period for which it is made and be made by notice in writing to the Inland Revenue not later that two years after the end of the accounting period to which it relates.

If the company is not entitled to R&D tax credit for the qualifying expenditure the trading loss is 150% of the pre-trading qualifying expenditure.

These are the rules that apply where a company has treated pre-trading qualifying expenditure as a trading loss

- The company cannot treat that expenditure as incurred on the first day of trading.

- The company cannot carry back the pre-trading loss to set against profits of an earlier accounting period unless it is entitled to relief for pre-trading vaccines research expenditure for that earlier period.

- When the company starts to trade it can treat the pre-trading loss as a trading loss brought forward to the extent that it has not already had relief for the loss or surrendered it as group relief.

Tax credit

An SME can claim a tax credit, which is known as a vaccines tax credit (VTC), if it is entitled to VRR for an accounting period and has a trading loss or a pre-trading loss for that accounting period. When it claims VTC it receives a payment in exchange for the loss. The amount of the loss that may be surrendered in exchange for a payment of tax credit is called a surrenderable loss.

The surrenderable loss for an accounting period is the lower of the unrelieved trading loss for that period and the VRR for that period.

The unrelieved trading loss for an accounting period is the trading loss for that period less

– any amounts that could have been set against other income of that period and

– any losses relieved in some other way, for example by being carried back against profits of an earlier accounting period.

Any losses brought forward from earlier accounting periods or carried back from later accounting periods are ignored.

Example

Drugs on Demand Plc is entitled to VRR of £4 million for its accounts year ended 30 June 2003. It has losses brought forward £2 million and a trading loss of £3 million for that year. This means that its unrelieved trading loss is £3 million. The losses brought forward of £2 million are ignored. Its surrenderable loss is £3 million because that is the lower of its unrelieved trading loss, £3 million, and the VRR, £4 million.

If a SME company claims VTC the Inland Revenue pays it the amount of the credit, at a rate of 16%, subject to the same conditions as for the SME R&D credit generally (see above).

How VRR is given: large companies

The rules are simpler for large companies (but they may not claim VTC).

The general rule is that when a company that is carrying on a trade is entitled to VRR the company may claim an additional deduction equal to 50% of the qualifying expenditure for an accounting period.

In the exceptional case where the qualifying expenditure is not deductible in its CT computations, the company may claim a deduction equal to 150% of the qualifying expenditure for the accounting period. For example, a company may incur expenditure on contributing to independent vaccines research that is relevant R&D but is not incurred wholly & exclusively for the purposes of its trade. If so, the company may deduct 150% of its qualifying expenditure in the accounting period in which it is incurred.

How VRR is given : insurance companies

There are special rules for taxing insurance companies and so there are special rules for VRR for them. They apply where the company's profits from life assurance business are taxed under Case III, V or VI Schedule D rather than Case I. If the company is taxed Case I Schedule D the normal rules apply.

Refunds of payments or contributions

A company that has made payments for sub-contracted R&D or made contributions to independent R&D may receive a refund of all or part of the payment or contribution.

51   Profit Computations

If it does, the appropriate amount is treated as Case I income.

For SMEs the appropriate amount is

- 50% of the refund where the payment qualified for R&D tax credits for SMEs,

and

- 150% of the refund in other cases.

For large companies the appropriate amount is

- 50% of the refund where the payment could be deducted in computing trading profits,

and

- 150% of the refund in other cases.

Specified diseases

Only research and development (see [below]) into vaccines and medicines for the prevention and treatment of certain diseases in humans qualifies for VRR. The specified diseases are tuberculosis, malaria and HIV/ AIDS.

- Qualifying R&D may relate either to vaccines or to drugs, for either prevention (prophylactic) or treatment (therapeutic) of **Tuberculosis**

- Qualifying R&D activity may include vaccines or medicines for **Malaria**, either prophylactic or therapeutic. Research into new or improved preventative medicines will qualify even if the principal beneficiaries are travellers to non-infected areas.

- R&D activity into **HIV/ AIDs** will qualify for relief if it is directed towards:

  - Vaccines for the prevention of infection by HIV,

  or

  - Vaccines or medicines for the prevention of the onset, or the treatment, of AIDS resulting from infection by HIV in clades (sub-types of the virus) A,C,D or E only. (Note that, whilst vaccines will normally be clade specific, there is no restriction to the relief by reference to the clades in the case of prophylactic vaccines. Anti- retroviral medicines are not clade specific, and so research or development aimed at these will not qualify for relief.)

The Treasury has powers by Regulation, to vary the prescribed clades, and to make provision further defining the qualifying R&D activity. These powers are necessary because particularly the HIV virus continues to mutate. However the number of specified diseases cannot be increased by Regulations.

Research into any of these is qualifying R&D activity and qualifies for VRR provided that the other conditions are satisfied

THE DEFINITION OF "RESEARCH AND DEVELOPMENT"

A new definition of R&D for tax purposes was introduced by Section 68 and Schedule 19 FA 2000 and has effect from 1st April 2000.

An activity will qualify as R&D for tax purposes if it would be treated as R&D under normal accounting practice for companies in the UK (Statement of Standard Accountancy Practice 13, SSAP13), as qualified by the "Guidelines on the Meaning of Research and Development for Tax Purposes" (see http://www.dti.gov.uk/support/taxcredit_b.htm) issued by the Secretary of State for Trade and Industry.

The Guidelines have statutory force. They discuss in detail the meaning of R&D, and illustrate through explanation and examples the boundary between those activities that are, and are not R&D.

Broadly speaking, an activity may qualify as R&D if it is characterised by work that contains an appreciable element of innovation and creativity in the fields of science and technology. The work can range from research into purely theoretical areas to applied research and experimental development directed towards a practical aim or product. It is research that aims to break new ground or to resolve scientific or technological uncertainties.

R&D is "creative work undertaken on a systematic basis in order to increase the stock of knowledge...and the use of this knowledge to devise new applications." For an activity to qualify it must meet three criteria

● it must seek to achieve a scientific or technological advancement

● it must seek to resolve a scientific or technological uncertainty

● it must be by way of systematic investigation.

R&D can include the development of prototypes and pilot plant to test the R&D, but commercial development without such scientific or technological investigation, or after the resolution of such uncertainties, is not R&D for tax purposes.

OTHER DEFINITIONS

Staffing costs

Staffing costs are all amounts paid to directors and employees. In more detail, they are

● all money payments such as salaries, wages, fees and bonuses before deductions for PAYE, National Insurance, or other agreed sums (such as season ticket loans etc). But they do not include the costs of providing benefits in kind.

● the employer's National Insurance contributions paid in respect of the employee insofar as they relate to the money payments (Class 1 NIC). However, NIC on benefits in kind (Class 1A, Class 1B NIC) are excluded.

● all payments to a pension fund by the employer in respect of the company's directors or employees directly engaged in R&D to provide those R&D staff with a pension, retirement annuity or other superannuation benefits.

● recruitment costs and related personnel costs such as relocation expenses are not included. Payments to agencies for the provision of staff do not qualify.

Staffing costs attributable to relevant research and development are staffing costs paid to or in respect of, directors and employees directly and actively engaged in R&D.

People directly and actively engaged in R&D are those actually undertaking the R&D, staff providing technical support and managers who plan and organise the programme of research.

The costs of people more remotely involved such as those providing clerical or general administrative services are not staffing costs attributable to relevant research and development. These staff, despite being peripheral to the R&D, may be regarded as essential to the successful outcome of the activity. Nevertheless, their costs do not qualify.

Whether an employee is directly and actively engaged in R&D is a question of fact based on the duties performed and not on the job title.

"Directly and actively engaged" refers to hands on work. Hands-on work performed by an employee includes:

● preparing equipment and materials for experiments and analysis, but not maintaining equipment;

● experimentation and analysis;

51   Profit Computations

- recording measurements, making calculations, and preparing charts and graphs; and

- performing work with respect to engineering or design, operations research, mathematical analysis, computer programming, data collection.

Supervisors and managers

Supervisors and managers performing tasks such as described above as hands-on are also directly and actively engaged. In addition, time they spend directing the technical course of, or providing direct technical input into, the ongoing R&D activities can be considered as direct engagement in R&D. However, time they spend on non-technological management aspects of activities, such as long-term strategic planning, contract administration and other decision-making functions that do not directly influence the on-going R&D activities, is not considered direct engagement in R&D.

The following are examples of qualifying and non-qualifying staff connected with a R&D project in the electronics industry:

- Director of Research: would qualify in respect of time spent either in a hands-on capacity or in the management of the project.

- Director's Secretary: would not qualify, assuming involved only in general secretarial duties.

- Engineers: would qualify for work on the R&D project.

- Computer Programmers: would qualify for work on the R&D project.

- Maintenance Staff: would not qualify as they are not directly engaged in the R&D activity.

- Clerical Support Team: would not qualify even though the support they give to the engineers, programmers is essential.

- Data Input Staff: would qualify assuming they are directly involved in the project.

- Receptionist: would not qualify.

- Technical/Documentation Writer: would not qualify as this work relates to the commercial or product development.

If staff spend only part of their time on R&D, costs should be apportioned to arrive at the qualifying staff costs. If an employee spends more than 80% of his or her time on R&D, the whole cost qualifies. Conversely, if an employee spends less than 20% of his or her time on R&D none of the cost qualifies. These percentages are by reference to the accounting period.

Consumable stores

Expenditure on consumable stores is expenditure on materials and equipment used up in the R&D activity, but which are not in themselves incorporated or reflected in the product of the R&D. Supplies, materials, or equipment used only indirectly in the R&D effort e.g. related to general overheads such as administration will not qualify.

Consumable stores are, by their nature comparatively short-lived, and spending on them will be revenue expenditure. For example, the consumable stores of a chemistry-based R&D project may include such items as disposable laboratory equipment (flasks, test tubes) and chemicals used in the R&D process, etc. This spending will be revenue expenditure and could qualify for R&D tax relief. But expenditure on a centrifuge will usually be on capital account, and will not qualify.

Expenditure on heat, light, power, rent, rates, interest, lease payments are not consumable stores.

74

Some consumable stores are recyclable; for example, it may be economically viable to sell the waste products from chemicals used in an R&D activity. The whole cost of such items can still be claimed as qualifying for the R&D tax relief.

Relevant research and development

Relevant research and development for a company is research and development

- related to a trade that the company carries on, or

- from which it is intended that a trade to be carried on by the company will be derived.

R&D related to a trade includes:

- any R&D which may lead to or facilitate an extension of the trade; and

- medical research which has a special relation to the welfare of workers employed in that trade, for example research into an occupational disease.

"Medical research which has a special relation to the welfare of workers employed in a trade" does not include research undertaken for the benefit of the community as a whole unless, of course, it is pursued by a company whose trade includes developing new pharmaceuticals.

Qualifying bodies

A qualifying body is a charity, an institution of higher education such as a university, a scientific research organisation or a health service body. All of these classes are defined in legislation, and apply to the UK only. In addition, the Treasury may, by order, add individual bodies or classes of bodies to the list of qualifying bodies. A list of those bodies which have been so designated will be kept on the Inland Revenue website.

Notified State aid

A notified State aid is a State aid which has been notified to, and approved by, the European Commission.

Notified state aids are usually government funded grants such as the SMART award, but not all government grants are notified State aids — for example, some funding under the SMART label is not notified State aid (e.g. grants for feasibility studies and microenterprise awards).

Sometimes companies carry out work that is funded directly by an initiative of the European Community. As the funding is not provided by a Member State, it cannot be notified State aid. So although receipt of such funding will constitute a subsidy and so reduce the amount of expenditure for which a company can claim, for example, the SME tax relief, it does not disallow it completely (unless the project is 100% subsidised).

If clarification of the status of a grant is needed, the body that has provided or arranged the funds should be able to help.

ARTIFICIALLY INFLATED CLAIMS

There is anti-avoidance legislation to prevent a company getting more R&D tax relief than it would normally be entitled to.

R&D tax relief is not due for a transaction that forms part of arrangements entered into wholly of mainly for a disqualifying purpose.

Arrangements are entered into wholly of mainly for a disqualifying purpose if their object, or one of their main objects, is to let a company obtain more R&D tax relief than it would otherwise be entitled to.

Arrangements are widely defined to include any scheme, agreement or understanding, whether or not it is legally enforceable.

HOW TO CLAIM R&D TAX RELIEF

To obtain the R&D tax reliefs, including payable R&D or vaccines tax credit, a company must make a claim in its tax return, form CT600. It would be useful if the accompanying computations provide a breakdown of the amount claimed and give a brief synopsis, in layman's terms, of the activities and the basis on which they constitute R&D.

The claim may be made, amended or withdrawn at any time up to the first anniversary of the filing date for the return for the accounting period for which the claim is made.

Interest is payable on a payable R&D tax credit from the later of

● the filing date for the accounting period for which the claim is made, and

● the date on which the return or amended return containing the claim was delivered to the inland Revenue

until the date payment is made.

You may find it helpful to discuss the claim with the Inspector beforehand, especially if this is the company's first claim for any of the R&D reliefs.'

52   Purchase by a Company of its Own Shares

52.6   **Clearance procedure.** It is noted that applications for clearance should now be addressed to Mohini Sawhney, Fifth Floor, 22 Kingsway, London WC2B 6NR (or, if market-sensitive information is included, to Ray McCann at that address). Applications may be faxed to 020–7438 4409 or e-mailed to reconstructions@gtnet.gov.uk (after advising Ray McCann (on 020–7438 6585) if market-sensitive information is included). Application may now be made in a single letter to the same address for clearance under *ICTA 1988, s 225* and under any one or more of *ICTA 1988, s 215* (demergers, see 29.57 GROUPS OF COMPANIES), *ICTA 1988, s 707* (transactions in securities, see Tolley's Income Tax under Anti-Avoidance), *TCGA 1992, s 138(1)* (share exchanges, see Tolley's Capital Gains Tax under Anti-Avoidance), *TCGA 1992, s 139(5)* (reconstructions involving the transfer of a business, see 9.6 CAPITAL GAINS), *TCGA 1992, s 140B* (transfer of a UK trade between EC Member States, see 9.8 CAPITAL GAINS), *TCGA 1992, s 140D* (transfer of non-UK trade between EC Member States, see 9.9 CAPITAL GAINS) and *FA 2002, Sch 29 para 88* (see 38.26 INTANGIBLE ASSETS).

54   Residence

54.1,   **Residence.** The note at the end of each of these sections is revised as follows.
54.2

'**Note.** For DOUBLE TAX RELIEF (21) purposes, the definition of residence will often be affected by the terms of the relevant agreement. For the circumstances in which the Revenue will certify that a company is UK resident for the purposes of double tax agreements, see Revenue Tax Bulletin December 2002, pp 989–991.'

See 21.3 above for the full text of the Revenue Tax Bulletin article referred to.

54.4   **Non-resident companies.** The following final paragraph is added.

'**Note.** With effect for accounting periods (of non-resident companies) beginning on or after 1 January 2003, legislation is to be introduced (in the 2003 Finance Bill) replacing the reference to carrying on a trade in the UK through a branch or agency with a reference to carrying on a trade in the UK through a "permanent establishment" (a definition of which is to be provided). The profits attributable to a permanent establishment in the UK are to be specially defined as those which would have been made had the permanent establishment been a distinct and separate enterprise dealing wholly independently with the non-resident company. In particular, the assumption will be made that the permanent establishment has the equity capital it would have had in those circumstances, and correspondingly lower loan capital, thus denying relief for excessive payments of interest to the non-resident company. See Revenue Press Release REV BN 25, 17 April 2002 and, for draft clauses, Revenue Press Release 27 November 2002.'

54.7   **Company becoming non-resident: notice of intention to cease residence.** It is noted that the address for notifications (within 54.7(*a*)) is now Mark Ritchie, Inland Revenue, Revenue Policy, International, Business Tax Group (Company Migrations), Victory House, 30–34 Kingsway, London WC2B 6ES.

---

56   Self-Assessment

56.7   **Enquiry into return.** The following paragraph is added.

'*Enquiry framework*. In March 2002, the Revenue published a framework within which income tax self-assessment enquiries will be worked and to which professional advisers are encouraged to adhere. Particular topics covered are the opening enquiry letter, requests for and conduct of interviews and meetings, and requests for non-business bank and building society accounts (plus credit/charge/store card details). (Revenue "Working Together" Bulletin No 8, March 2002). A similar framework, suitably adapted, applies to corporation tax self-assessment enquiries. See Revenue "Working Together" Bulletin No 12, March 2003.'

56.14   **Company tax return.** It is noted that the supplementary pages with Form CT600 (2002) are as follows.

'CT600A   *Loans to participators by close companies.* This must be completed if the company is a close company and made loans to an individual participator, or associate of a participator, that remained outstanding at the end of the period. See 13.9 *et seq.* CLOSE COMPANIES.

CT600B   *Controlled foreign companies.* This must be completed if the company had an interest of 25% or more in the period in a foreign company which was controlled from the UK. See 18 CONTROLLED FOREIGN COMPANIES. See also section 2.1 of the Revenue Guidance Notes referred to at 18.1 as regards completion of these supplementary pages.

CT600C   *Group and consortium companies.* This must be completed if the company is claiming or surrendering any amounts under the group or consortium relief provisions or any eligible unrelieved foreign tax for the period. See 29.14 *et seq.* GROUPS OF COMPANIES, 21.6 DOUBLE TAX RELIEF.

CT600D   *Insurance companies and friendly societies.* This must be completed if, in the period, the company either made claims under *ICTA 1988, Sch 19AB* to provisional payments (including notional repayments in respect of tax on gilt interest) (see 42.6 LIFE INSURANCE COMPANIES), or entered into business which it treats as overseas life assurance business (see 42.14 LIFE INSURANCE COMPANIES).

CT600E   *Charities and community amateur sports clubs.* This must be completed if the company is, in the period, a charity or community amateur sports club claiming exemption or partial exemption from tax. See 11 CHARITIES, 63.8 VOLUNTARY ASSOCIATIONS.

CT600F   *Tonnage tax.* This must be completed where an election has been made for the alternative tonnage tax regime (see 51.28 PROFIT COMPUTATIONS).

CT600G   *Corporate venturing scheme.* This must be completed if the company is claiming relief under the CORPORATE VENTURING SCHEME (19).

CT600H   *Cross-border royalties.* This must be completed if the company made cross-border royalty payments after 1 October 2002 without deduction of tax or under deduction of tax at a treaty-specified rate (see 31.3 INCOME TAX IN RELATION TO A COMPANY).

CT600I   *Supplementary charge in respect of ring fence trades.* This must be completed if the company carried on a ring fence trade in a period beginning (or deemed to have begun) after 16 April 2002. See 47.3 OIL COMPANIES.'

60   Unit and Investment Trusts

60.1   **Authorised unit trusts: futures and options.** A reference is added to an article in the Revenue Tax Bulletin (August 2002 p 949) concerning the underlying reasons for the repeal of *ICTA 1988, s 468AA.*

For the text of the Revenue Tax Bulletin article referred to, see 25.11 FINANCIAL INSTRUMENTS AND DERIVATIVE CONTRACTS.

61   Value Added Tax

61.6   A new section is added as follows.

'**FLAT RATE SCHEME**

An optional VAT flat rate scheme was introduced as *VATA 1994, s 26B* by *FA 2002, s 23*. The scheme is available to all businesses with a VAT-exclusive annual taxable turnover of up to £100,000 in the year of entry to the scheme, and with a VAT-exclusive turnover, including the value of exempt supplies and other non-taxable income, of up to £125,000. For the Revenue view as to how profits chargeable under Schedule D, Case I or II are to be computed by businesses adopting the scheme, see Revenue Tax Bulletin October 2002 pp 973, 974.'

The text of the Revenue Tax Bulletin article referred to is as below.

'**VALUE ADDED TAX — FLAT RATE SCHEME**

1. Computation Of Profits Case I/II Schedule D

2. Service Companies ("IR35") Legislation — Deemed Payment Calculation

An optional VAT flat rate scheme was introduced with effect from 24 April 2002 by FA2002/S23. The scheme is available to all businesses with a VAT exclusive annual taxable turnover of up to £100,000 in the year of entry to the scheme, and with a VAT exclusive turnover, including the value of exempt supplies and other non taxable income, of up to £125,000.

A business that joins the scheme avoids having to account internally for VAT on all purchases and supplies, and instead calculates its net liability by applying a flat rate percentage to the tax inclusive turnover. The flat rate percentage depends upon the trade sector into which a business falls for the purposes of the scheme. Full details of the scheme are included in VAT Notice 733 Flat rate scheme for small businesses, which is available on the internet at www.hmce.gov.uk/forms/notices/733.htm or in printed form by telephoning 0845 010 9000.

1. Computation Of Profits Case I/II Schedule D

Our view on how profits chargeable under Case I/II of Schedule D are to be computed by businesses who adopt the scheme is as follows.

Businesses draw up their accounts on the VAT exclusive or on the VAT inclusive basis. Which ever method is used will result in the same profits being charged under Case I/II of Schedule D over the lifetime of the business.

Where the exclusive accounting basis is used

All VAT on inputs and outputs,including the amount due under the flat rate scheme, is taken to a separate VAT account. In the financial statements any balance on that account at the accounting date in respect of VAT, which cannot be recovered from HM Customs and Excise, is debited to the profit and loss account (where it is likely to be included in either administration costs or with other operating costs). The VAT not recovered is an allowable expense in computing the business profits for the purposes of Case I and II of Schedule D.

Any balance on the account that is an excess of VAT that is not due to be paid over to HM Customs and Excise, is credited to the profit and loss account (where it is likely to be included with other operating income or deducted from expenses). This is a taxable receipt of the business for the purposes of Case I and II of Schedule D. The reason for this is that VAT is an incidental cost of being in business. The gross payments from customers are received in the course of business and any VAT element included in those payments that does not have to be paid over to HM Customs and Excise does not lose that business nature.

Example 1

A business has sales, net of VAT, of £80,000, with VAT received from customers of £14,000 (£80,000 x 17.5%), giving gross sales of £94,000. Expenses, net of VAT, total £50,000, with VAT paid on expenses of £8,750 (£50,000 x 17.5%). A new machine is purchased (qualifying for capital allowances) at a cost of £2,350, including VAT of £350. Flat rate VAT is paid to HM Customs and Excise of £5,640 (£94,000 x 6%).

VAT account

	DR £	CR £
VAT collected on sales		14,000
VAT paid on expenses	8,750	
Flat rate scheme VAT paid	5,640	
VAT paid on machine	350	
Profit and loss account		740
	14,740	14,740

61 Value Added Tax

Case I profit computation

Sales	£80,000
Expenses (including "irrecoverable" VAT £740)	£50,740
Case I profit	£29,260

Qualifying expenditure for capital allowances £2,000 (£2,350 – £350)

Example 2

As Example 1 but expenses net of VAT, total £40,000, with VAT paid of £7,000 (£40,000 x 17.5%).

VAT account

	DR £	CR £
VAT collected on sales		14,000
VAT paid on expenses	7,000	
Flat rate scheme VAT paid	5,640	
VAT paid on machine	350	
Profit and loss account	1,010	
	14,000	14,000

Case I profit computation

Sales	£80,000
Other operating income – surplus VAT	£1,010
	£81,010
Expenses	£40,000
Case I profit	£41,010

Qualifying expenditure for capital allowances £2,000

Where the inclusive accounting basis is used

Turnover will include all the VAT charged to customers but it should exclude the amount paid to HM Customs and Excise under the flat rate scheme. Expenses will include all VAT paid on those expenses.

For example, taking the same figures used in the previous Example 1 above:

Sales (£80,000 + VAT £14,000 charged to customers)	£94,000
Less flat rate VAT	£5,640
	£88,360
Expenses (£50,000 + VAT £8,750)	£58,750
Case I profit	£29,610

Qualifying expenditure for capital allowances £2,350

2. Service Companies ("IR35") Legislation — Deemed Payment Calculation

The amount to be included under Step 1 of the deemed payment calculation is the VAT exclusive amount whether or not the Flat Rate scheme is adopted.'

62   Venture Capital Trusts

62.1   **Introduction.** It is noted that the new Revenue Venture Capital Schemes Manual ('VCM') has been published, dealing *inter alia* with Venture Capital Trusts. A general cross-reference to VCM 10000 – 17320, VCM 60000 *et seq.* is inserted. Other references to the Inspector's Manual ('IM') in this chapter are accordingly amended to the corresponding reference in the new Manual. See 62.3 below.

62.2   **Conditions for approval.** The section on *Share exchanges and conversions* is renamed *Company restructuring and share conversions* and the following text added.

'Where, after 20 March 2000 under a company reorganisation, takeover or scheme of reconstruction,

- a VCT exchanges a qualifying holding for other shares or securities (with or without other consideration), and

- the exchange is for *bona fide* commercial reasons and not part of a tax avoidance scheme or arrangements,

regulations provide a formula which values the new shares or securities, for the purposes of the 70%, 30% and 15% tests in (*b*) and (*d*) above, by reference to the proportion of the value of the old shares or securities that the market value of the new shares or securities bears to the total consideration receivable. If no other consideration is receivable, the value of the new is identical to that of the old. The provisions extend to new shares or securities received in pursuance of an earn-out right (see Tolley's Capital Gains Tax under Shares and Securities) conferred in exchange for a qualifying holding, in which case an election is available (under *Reg 10*) to modify the formula by effectively disregarding the earn-out right itself. [*SI 2002 No 2661*].'

62.3   **Qualifying holdings.** As referred to at 91.1 above, references to the Revenue Inspector's Manual are replaced with references to the new Venture Capital Schemes Manual, as follows.

Paragraph	Old reference	New reference
91.3(*b*)	IM 6982, IM 7204	VCM 15070, VCM 62310
	IM 7001	VCM 17310
	IM 6983, IM 7204	VCM 17040
91.3(*c*)	IM 6975A, IM 7197, IM 7197B	VCM 12080, VCM 62150–62153

Also, the penultimate paragraph of the section ('To deal with cases where shares or securities ...') is replaced with the following.

'Where, after 20 March 2000 under a company reorganisation, takeover or scheme of reconstruction,

- a VCT exchanges a qualifying holding for other shares or securities (with or without other consideration), and

- the exchange is for *bona fide* commercial reasons and not part of a tax avoidance scheme or arrangements,

the new shares or securities may be treated as being qualifying holdings for a specified period even if some or all of the above requirements are not otherwise satisfied. Regulations specify the circumstances in which, and conditions subject to which, they apply and which requirements are to be treated as met. Where the new shares or securities are those of a different company than before and they do not meet any one or more of the above requirements (disregarding (*c*) and (*d*)), those requirements are treated as met for, broadly, three years in the case of shares or five years in the case of securities, reduced in either case to, broadly, two years where the company is not, or ceases to be, an unquoted company as in (*a*) above. A formula is provided for valuing the new shares or securities for the purposes of (*j*) above. The provisions extend to new shares or securities received in pursuance of an earn-out right (see Tolley's Capital Gains Tax under Shares and Securities) conferred in exchange for a qualifying holding, in which case an election is available (under *Reg 10*) to modify the said valuation formula by effectively disregarding the earn-out right itself. [*SI 2002 No 2661*].'

Budget Summary 9 April 2003

Note: *It must be remembered that these proposals are subject to amendment during the passage of the Finance Bill.*

PERSONAL TAXATION	2003/04	2002/03
Personal allowance		
general	£4,615	£4,615
aged 65 or over in year		
of assessment	£6,610	£6,100
aged 75 or over in year		
of assessment	£6,720	£6,370
age allowance income limit	£18,300	£17,900
minimum where income		
exceeds limit	£4,615	£4,615
Married couple's allowance		
(10% relief)		
either spouse born before		
6 April 1935	£5,565	£5,465
either spouse aged 75 or over		
in year of assessment	£5,635	£5,535
age allowance income limit	£18,300	£17,900
minimum where income		
exceeds limit	£2,150	£2,110
Blind person's allowance	£1,510	£1,480
Children's tax credit		
(10% relief, income-related)		
basic	—	£5,290
year of birth	—	£10,490
Income tax rates		
Starting rate	10%	10%
on taxable income up to	£1,960	£1,920
Basic rate	22%	22%
on taxable income from		
starting rate limit up to	£30,500	£29,900
Higher rate	40%	40%
on taxable income over	£30,500	£29,900
Lower rate		
on certain interest income	20%	20%

COMPANY TAXATION	FY2003	FY2002
Corporation tax rates		
All companies (except below)	30%	30%
Companies with small profits	19%	19%
– 19% rate limit	£300,000	£300,000
– marginal relief limit	£1,500,000	£1,500,000
– marginal rate	32.75%	32.75%
Starting rate	0%	0%
– 0% rate limit	£10,000	£10,000
– marginal relief limit	£50,000	£50,000
– marginal rate	23.75%	23.75%

CAPITAL GAINS TAX	2003/04	2002/03
Rate — general	10%*:20%*:40%	*10%*:20%*:40%*
— trustees and personal		
representatives	34%*	34%*
General exemption limit	£7,900	£7,700
*subject to tapering relief in certain cases		

INHERITANCE TAX	Transfers after 5/4/2003
Threshold	£255,000
Death rate	40%

VAT

Standard rate	17.5%
Registration threshold after 9 April 2003	£56,000
(previously £55,000 after 24 April 2002)	

NATIONAL INSURANCE 2003/04

(2002/03 in brackets where different)

Class 1 Contributions

Not contracted out

The employee contribution is 11% (10%) of earnings between £89 and £595 (£585) p.w. plus 1% of all earnings above £595 p.w. (no liability arising for 2002/03 on earnings above £585 p.w.).

The employer contribution is 12.8% (11.8%) of all earnings in excess of the first £89 p.w..

Contracted out

The 'not contracted out' rates for employees are reduced on the band of earnings from £89 p.w. to £595 (£585) p.w. by 1.6%. For employers, they are reduced on the band of earnings from £89 p.w. to £595 (£585) p.w. by 3.5% for employees in salary-related schemes or 1.0% for employees in money purchase schemes. In addition, there is an employee rebate of 1.6% and an employer rebate of 3.5% or 1.0%, as appropriate, on earnings from £77 (£75) p.w. up to £89 p.w..

Class 1A and 1B contributions	12.8%	(11.8%)

Class 2 contributions

Flat weekly rate		£2.00
Exemption limit	£4,095	(£4,025)

Class 3 contributions

Flat weekly rate	£6.95	(£6.85)

Class 4 contributions

8% (7%) on the band of profits between £4,615 and £30,940 (£30,420) *plus* 1% on all profits above £30,940 (no liability arising for 2002/03 on profits above £30,420).

Budget Summary

PERSONAL TAXATION

Income Tax Rates and Allowances

For 2003/04, the lower, basic and higher rates of income tax remain at 10%, 22% and 40% respectively.

The starting rate band is increased by £40 to £1,960, and the basic rate band by £560 to £28,540 (so that the higher rate applies to taxable income in excess of £30,500).

The special rates applicable to dividends and other savings income and the rates applicable to trusts are unchanged.

As announced in the Pre-Budget Report in November 2002, the personal allowance remains unchanged at £4,615. As previously announced, children's tax credit is abolished and replaced by the new 'child tax credit', which varies according to income and circumstances, is paid direct to the main carer and is not related to income tax liability. For other personal reliefs (which were also announced in the Pre-Budget Report), see the Table at the front of this summary.

Pension Schemes Earnings Cap

From 6 April 2003, the maximum level of earnings for which pension provision may be made under tax-approved occupational and personal pension schemes is increased by £1,800 to £99,000. New legislation, effective from 9 April 2003, will put beyond doubt the fact that both employee and employer contributions to a personal pension scheme are subject to this earnings cap.

Car Fuel Benefit

As previously announced, for 2003/04 onwards, fuel scale charges for employees receiving free fuel for private (including home to work) mileage in company cars are replaced by a new system. The percentage used to calculate the benefit of the company car itself, which is based on CO_2 emissions and varies between 15% and 35% for petrol cars, is applied to a figure of £14,400, and the result is taken as the value of the car fuel benefit. It thus varies between £2,160 and £5,040. The set percentages are each increased by 3 points for diesel cars (subject to a maximum of 35%) and there are discounts for alternative fuelled cars. As before, no charge applies if the employee is required to make good to the employer the cost of all fuel used for private purposes and does, in fact, do so. The value of the benefit is now proportionately reduced if this condition begins to be met, or fuel ceases to be provided for private use, from a date partway through the tax year, provided this then continues to be the case for the rest of the tax year. It is also proportionately reduced if the car is not available for part of the tax year.

Employer-provided Vans

The Government has announced a consultation on proposals to reform the tax treatment of employer-provided vans to take account of environmental benefits, fairness and modern working practices. (The current flat rate charge is £500 (£350 where at least four years old) for exclusive use. Charges on shared vans are shared between participating employees, or they can opt for a daily charge of £5.)

Employee Benefits

Proposals have been made to increase the exemption limits in respect of the following employee benefits in kind from the date the amending regulations come into force.

Long service awards. Currently a tax-free award (other than cash) can be made to an employee with a minimum of 20 years service with the employer up to a value of £20 for each year of service. This limit is to be increased to £50. Such additional tax-free gifts can be awarded for each further period of ten years service.

Christmas parties and other annual functions. Currently an annual party or similar celebration paid for by the employer and open to employees generally is exempt from tax where the cost is no more than £75 per head per year. This limit is to be doubled to £150.

84

Gifts from third parties. Gifts (other than cash) made to employees by third parties (i.e. other than the employer) are exempt from tax where the total value of such gifts made in a tax year is £150 or less. This limit is to be increased to £250.

Meals for those who cycle to work. Meals or refreshments can currently be provided tax-free on up to six occasions a year to employees who participate in official cycle to work days. It is proposed that this limit be removed.

Financial Support to Adopters

Proposed legislation will ensure that financial support to adopters by local authorities and adoption agencies will continue to be free of tax.

Adoption allowances are currently free of tax under extra-statutory concession (ESC A40). However, this does not apply to payments under the Adoption and Children Act 2002, so new legislation will put the tax exemption of all adoption payments onto a statutory footing.

Foster Carers

Individuals who provide foster care services to local authorities, either directly or through an agency, are taxable on any profit they make. It is proposed that, for 2003/04 onwards, a foster carer whose gross receipts from foster care do not exceed an individual limit will be treated as having a nil profit and nil loss from foster care for the tax year concerned. Foster carers whose gross receipts from foster care exceed their individual limit will have the choice of being taxed on that excess or computing their profit or loss from foster care using the normal rules for calculating business profits and losses. The individual limit is made up of a fixed amount of £10,000 per residence for a full tax year and an additional amount per child for each week, or part week, that the individual provides foster care. These amounts are £200 per week for a child under 11 and £250 per week for a child of 11 or over.

Giving to Charities

As provided for in FA 2002, s 98 for gifts made under Gift Aid after 5 April 2003, donors may elect to have the donation treated as though made in the previous year of assessment.

It is now proposed that from April 2004, taxpayers can nominate a charity to receive all or part of any tax repayments due to them. The nomination would be made on the taxpayer's self-assessment return for 2003/04 and later years, with an indication of whether Gift Aid should apply to the donation. The Inland Revenue will pass the donation direct to the charity.

As announced in the Pre-Budget Report in November 2002 the 10% government supplement on donations to charities made through the Payroll Giving scheme will be extended for a further year until 5 April 2004.

Personal Service Companies etc: Domestic Workers

Domestic workers, such as nannies or butlers, who provide their services via an intermediary (usually a personal service company) are to be brought within the so-called IR 35 rules, under which workers who *would* be employees if engaged directly rather than through a company or other intermediary are effectively taxed (and charged national insurance) as if they *were* employees. The extension of these rules to domestic workers applies, for income tax purposes, to income received by the intermediary in respect of services provided by the worker after 9 April 2003. For national insurance purposes, however, the extension will apply only to income received by the intermediary in respect of services provided on or after the day that proposed new Regulations take effect; these Regulations are expected to be introduced in the summer of 2003. These different start dates could mean that, for 2003/04 only, separate calculations are required for income tax and national insurance purposes.

Home-working

With effect from 6 April 2003, it is proposed that employers may contribute towards additional household costs incurred by an employee who works some or all of the time at home under agreed

Budget Summary

flexible working arrangements, without it giving rise to a charge to income tax. Such payments can currently be made without giving rise to a NICs liability.

Employers will be able to pay up to £2 per week (£104 per year) without the need for supporting evidence of the costs the employee has incurred. Where the employer pays more than that amount, evidence will be required in order to obtain the exemption that the payment is wholly in respect of additional household expenses incurred by the employee in carrying out his duties at home.

Lloyd's Underwriters

Currently, Lloyd's Underwriters are not permitted to carry forward unused losses when they convert from Names into limited liability entities. This is in contrast to other traders who transfer a business to a company. To remove this disadvantage to the reform of Lloyd's it is proposed that Finance Bill 2004 will allow Names to carry forward unused trading losses when they convert. In addition, discussions will also focus on whether capital gains tax reliefs, that are available when businesses are transferred to a company, are effective in the case of Lloyd's Underwriters.

Claims and Elections Following Self-assessment Enquiries

For enquiries concluded from the date of Royal Assent to Finance Act 2003, self-assessment taxpayers will be given rights to make, amend and withdraw claims and elections at the end of an enquiry into a return, in line with the rights they enjoy where a 'discovery' assessment is made.

Residence and Domicile

A background paper has been published reviewing the residence and domicile rules as they affect the taxation of individuals.

Anti-avoidance: Relevant Discounted Securities

As previously announced, legislation is to be introduced, effective from 27 March 2003, to counter avoidance by individuals attempting to exploit the relevant discounted securities rules to create artificial income tax losses, and to remove the potential for tax to distort investment decisions between investment in such securities and normal interest-bearing securities. Certain special rules applying to gilt strips are to be expanded to apply to strips of non-UK government securities.

CORPORATION TAX

Corporation Tax Rates

For financial year 2003, the full, small companies' and starting rates of corporation tax remain at 30%, 19% and 0% respectively. The bands for the small companies' and starting rates, and hence the marginal reliefs, also remain unchanged. See the Table at the front of this summary. The full rate will remain at 30% for financial year 2004.

Interest on Overdue Employer and Contractor Liabilities

With effect for accounting periods ending on or after 9 April 2003, revisions are to be made to legislation to formalise current and accepted practice whereby interest incurred on overdue payments of tax, NICs, student loans, etc. is usually non-deductible in calculating income or profits for tax purposes.

Treasury Shares

Under new regulations, companies which purchase their own shares will, in future, be able to hold them and either sell them back into the market or cancel them. Shares held in this way are called 'Treasury Shares'.

For tax purposes shares will be treated as cancelled when bought and newly issued when sold. While held in treasury, they will be treated as if they do not exist.

At present, when companies buy their own shares, they must be cancelled. The purchase does not result in the company acquiring assets; new shares come into existence on issue.

No income tax relief will be due to individual investors when a Venture Capital Trust issues shares sold out of treasury, which are treated as newly issued.

Research and Development Tax Credits

Changes are proposed to the R&D tax credits to make it easier for companies, especially smaller companies, to qualify for the credits. The proposals include:

- reducing the minimum expenditure on qualifying R&D from £25,000 to £10,000;

- the extension of the definition of 'staffing costs' to include workers paid through a third party and not taken on by the R&D company;

- the abolition of the rule for claiming staff costs where an employee spends less than 20% or more than 80% of their time on R&D, resulting in nil or 100% relief respectively, this rule to be replaced by simply apportioning staff costs; and

- the extension of the circumstances in which an SME can claim the large company credit (since the SME credit may not be available where it would result in the company receiving state aid in excess of the permitted maximum).

There is also to be consultation on the definition of R&D to provide greater clarity and to include a proposed extension of reliefs to cover licences for short-life, advanced software.

The changes for large companies will take effect from 9 April 2003 and those for SMEs when approval has been received from the European Commission.

Collective Investment Funds

Two changes are intended to make UK-Authorised Collective Investment Funds more competitive abroad. Both take effect on distributions or Inheritance Tax occasions of charge on or after 16 October 2002 and will apply to UK-Authorised Unit Trusts (AUTs) and Open-ended Investment Companies (OEICs).

- Overseas investors will no longer need to complete a 'not ordinarily resident' declaration to receive interest gross provided that the interest is paid:

    (a)   to a reputable intermediary and the fund has reasonable grounds for believing that payment can be made gross; or

    (b)   to unit/share holders that are companies or trustees of a unit trust scheme.

- Non-UK domiciled people, or trusts established by them, will no longer face a potential charge to IHT on such funds held by them.

Court Common Investment Funds

Changes are to be made to the tax rules governing Court Common Investment Funds (CCIFs). CCIFs are a form of unit trust set up by the Lord Chancellor as vehicles into which funds in court may be placed. They can currently only be held by the Accountant General on behalf of road accident victims, for instance.

The changes apply to people with funds held in a CCIF on or after 6 April 2003 and will allow more people to participate in the funds, including beneficiaries themselves.

Insolvency

Following the Enterprise Act 2002 it is necessary to make some technical changes to the tax rules that apply to companies in liquidation and administration.

Budget Summary

Currently when companies go into liquidation their accounting periods are automatically set to last 12 months each until the company is wound-up. For liquidations ending on or after the date of the introduction of the new administration rules, which is expected to be later in 2003, if the company ceases to be in liquidation without being wound-up, the 12-month rule will cease to have effect. Also, currently where companies go into administration there is no impact on the accounting periods of the company. For any company going into administration on or after the date of the introduction of the new administration rules, commencement of administration will be the start of a new accounting period and the date it comes out of administration will mark the end of an accounting period.

A 'proper officer' is the person who, for the purposes of the Inland Revenue, acts on behalf of a company in administration. For any administration period entered into on or after the date of the introduction of the new administration rules, the proper officer will be the administrator or where there is more than one it will be one of them by nomination by themselves or otherwise by the Inland Revenue.

Currently rules apply that enable companies in liquidation to calculate their tax liabilities based on the previous year's tax rates enabling them to settle the affairs of the company quickly. Similar rules will now apply to companies in administration, applying to administrations entered into on or after the date of the introduction of the new administration rules.

For any liquidation in place on or after 9 April 2003 the special rules applying to loan relationships between connected companies will only cease to apply while that company remains in liquidation.

Urban Regeneration Companies

Businesses will be able to treat contributions to the running costs of Urban Regeneration Companies as a tax-deductible expense against profits. Relief is available for contributions made on or after 1 April 2003.

Sale and Repurchase Agreements

A number of measures are proposed to the tax rules for sale and repurchase (repo) agreements undertaken by financial institutions to counter avoidance schemes and clarify uncertainties. The changes will ensure that:

- where a transaction is treated as a repo for tax purposes, all the repo tax provisions will apply and that where some repo rules are disapplied, all such rules are disapplied;

- a clear scheme is provided for dealing with foreign exchange gains and losses arising on the original sale price in the repo;

- the anti-avoidance rules that counter schemes, which effectively convert taxable interest into non-taxable dividends, apply not only where the repo buyer receives a real dividend but also where a manufactured dividend is received; and

- a deduction for a deemed manufactured payment cannot be increased by an amount equal to what would have been the dividend tax credit before the abolition of ACT.

The changes apply to repo deals agreed, and to manufactured payments deemed to be made, on or after 9 April 2003.

Loan Relationships and Derivative Contracts

Revisions are proposed to the rules for loan relationships in FA 1996 and for derivative contracts in FA 2002 to provide greater certainty and to tackle avoidance. The proposals will ensure that where such loans or contracts are transferred between group companies:

- profits cannot fall out of charge where mark-to-market accounting is used;

- the tax treatment of exchange gains and losses will follow the accounting treatment; and

- the current tax treatment is clarified in the case where such contracts are novated (where one group member takes over the rights and obligations of another group member by means of a new agreement).

The connected party rules are also to be amended to stop a loan relationship avoidance scheme which attempts to create an allowable deduction for interest or discount which is accrued but never paid.

The amendments are to apply where the date of transfer falls, or where interest payments become due and payable, or discount arises, on or after 9 April 2003.

CAPITAL ALLOWANCES

Enhanced Capital Allowances

A number of capital allowances measures are to be introduced.

Expenditure incurred by businesses on or after 1 April 2003 on designated plant or machinery which meets strict water saving or efficiency criteria will qualify for 100% first-year allowances. Initially, the enhanced allowances will be available only for expenditure on meters and monitoring equipment, flow controllers, leakage detection, and efficient toilets and taps. Details of the qualifying technologies and products will be published as the Water Technology List, to be available on the Internet at www.eca.gov.uk

The 100% first-year allowances available to small businesses for expenditure on information and communication technology (ICT), which were due to expire on 31 March 2003, are to be extended so that expenditure incurred on or before 31 March 2004 will qualify.

New technologies are to be added to the list of energy-efficient plant and machinery qualifying for 100% first-year allowances, from a date yet to be announced, expected to be later in 2003.

The company law definition of small and medium-sized companies is to be aligned with the European Union definition. The effect of this change will be to increase the number of businesses eligible for 40% first-year allowances on plant and machinery expenditure and 100% first-year allowances on ICT. Legislation to amend the definition will be enacted as soon as the revised EU definition is finalised.

Anti-avoidance

An anti-avoidance measure is to be introduced to deny a balancing allowance in cases where the proceeds from a balancing event (such as a sale of the asset on which allowances have been claimed) are less than they would otherwise have been as a result of a tax avoidance scheme. The measure applies to capital allowances for assured tenancies, agricultural buildings, flat conversion, industrial buildings and mineral extraction. The provision was first announced in the Pre-Budget Report and applies to balancing events occurring on or after 27 November 2002. Where the provision is applied, any purchaser of the asset will nevertheless be able to claim allowances only on the amount paid for the asset.

CAPITAL GAINS TAX

Annual Exempt Amount and Rates

For 2003/04, the annual exempt amount for individuals is increased by £200 to £7,900, the amount for most trusts being increased by £100 to £3,950. The 10%/20%/40% rate structure, and the 34% rate for trustees and personal representatives, are unchanged.

Budget Summary

Capital Gains Tax Simplification

Legislation is to be included in the Finance Bill to enact the following capital gains tax simplification measures.

For 2003/04 tax returns and subsequent years, individuals, trustees and personal representatives will not need to complete the capital gains tax pages of the return if the total of their chargeable gains, after applying taper relief, does not exceed their annual exempt amount unless either the total proceeds from the disposal of non-exempt assets in the year exceed four times the annual exempt amount *for individuals* or they have allowable losses to set off against the gains. Proceeds of disposals between husband and wife will not count towards the proceeds limit if the disposal is treated as giving rise to neither a gain nor a loss. These provisions replace the current rule under which, broadly, the capital gains tax pages of the return do not need to be completed where the chargeable gains do not exceed the applicable annual exempt amount and the total proceeds do not exceed twice that amount.

The definition of a 'business asset' for the purposes of taper relief is to be amended in relation to periods of ownership from 6 April 2004 onwards for disposals on or after that date. Everything that qualifies as a business asset under the current rules will continue to qualify, and in addition, assets used wholly or partly for the purposes of a trade carried on by an individual, the trustees of a settlement, the personal representatives of a deceased person or certain partnerships will qualify as business assets irrespective of whether the owner of the asset is involved in carrying on the trade. The relevant types of partnership are those whose members include an individual, a person acting in the capacity of a trustee of a settlement or a personal representative, a company which is a qualifying company for taper relief purposes by reference to the asset's owner, or a company which belongs to a trading group whose holding company is a qualifying company by reference to the asset's owner.

Taxpayers incurring a loss on or after 10 April 2003 on the disposal of a right to unascertainable deferred consideration will, if certain conditions are met, be able to elect to treat the loss as arising in an earlier tax year. This measure is intended to alleviate the problem which can arise where an asset is sold for a right to receive unascertainable deferred consideration, thereby giving rise to a chargeable gain by reference to the market value of the right. If the right is subsequently disposed of in a later tax year and a loss arises, that loss cannot be set off against the earlier gain since capital losses cannot be carried back. The election can only be made if the person incurring the loss did not acquire the right second-hand, the disposal in respect of which the right was received gave rise to a chargeable gain and that person had a capital gains tax liability for the tax year in which that disposal was made. Special rules will apply where there were part disposals of the original asset in different tax years.

The provisions under which an earn-out right obtained in exchange for shares or debentures is treated as a security for capital gains purposes (thereby enabling the gain on disposal to be rolled over) are to be amended so that they will apply automatically where the conditions are met, subject to an election being made to disapply them. Currently, an election is required in order to apply the provisions. This change applies to earn-out rights conferred on or after 10 April 2003.

As a further simplification measure, the Revenue are to publish guidance on the calculation of chargeable gains arising on the disposal of shares or units in unit trusts acquired via monthly savings schemes. The guidance will supplement that already given in Revenue Statement of Practice SP 2/99. The Revenue intend to publish the guidance in time to assist in the completion of 2002/03 tax returns.

Offshore Trusts

Anti-avoidance provisions are to be introduced to block an avoidance scheme designed to allow beneficiaries of offshore trusts to which capital gains have arisen to receive capital payments from the trust without incurring a capital gains tax liability. The scheme seeks to exploit legislation introduced by FA 2000 intended to block another avoidance scheme, known as the 'flip flop' scheme.

An anomaly arising from a simplification measure in FA 2002 is also to be corrected, so that where a beneficiary is chargeable under the FA 2000 anti-flip flop legislation, and the amount of the charge is reduced by an amount already charged on a settlor, the amount of the reduction is limited to the tapered amount rather than the untapered amount.

The new provisions will apply to capital payments made by trustees to beneficiaries on or after 9 April 2003.

Options and the Market Value Rule

Measures are to be introduced to reverse the effect of the recent Court of Appeal decision in *Mansworth v Jelley* [2003] STC 53. Following that decision, where assets are acquired via options granted otherwise than by way of a bargain at arm's length or by reason of employment, their acquisition cost is treated for capital gains purposes as the market value of the asset at the time the option is exercised. Likewise, the disposal proceeds of the person granting and satisfying the option are also treated as the market value at that time. In the case of shares acquired under certain unapproved employee share options, the acquisition cost may be further increased by any amount charged to income tax in respect of the exercise. For options exercised on or after 10 April 2003, the new measures will secure that this 'market value rule' will not apply to substitute market value for the actual amount payable when the option is exercised. As a result, on the exercise of such an option (other than an employee share option), the disposal proceeds of the person selling the asset, and the acquisition cost of the person acquiring it, will take into account the market value of the option at the time it was granted and the amount payable on exercise. In the case of an unapproved employee share option, the disposal proceeds will be the sum of the amount payable for the option and the amount payable on exercise and the employee's acquisition cost will be the same amount plus any amount charged to income tax on exercise.

INHERITANCE TAX

Threshold

The inheritance tax threshold is increased by £5,000 to £255,000 for tax charges arising on or after 6 April 2003.

SHARE SCHEMES

Employee Benefit Trusts

Proposed legislation published in draft form on 27 November 2002 is designed to 'counter the avoidance of tax and National Insurance Contributions through the abuse of employee benefit trusts'. It provides rules for the timing of deductions for 'employee benefit contributions'. To this extent, these rules replace the existing rules in FA 1989, ss 43, 44. They apply in relation to deductions otherwise allowable in computing profits for periods ending after 26 November 2002 in respect of contributions made after that date. For these purposes, an '*employee benefit contribution*' is a payment of money, or the transfer of an asset, by the employer to a third party (e.g. the trustees of an employee benefit trust) to be held or used to provide benefits to employees. A deduction is allowed only to the extent that, during the period in question or within nine months after the end of it, the contribution is used either to provide employee benefits chargeable (with certain exceptions) to both tax and National Insurance or to meet the third party's expenses in operating the scheme (to the extent that such expenses would have been deductible if incurred by the employer). Any amount thus disallowed remains available for deduction in any subsequent period during which it is used to provide such benefits. Where a benefit takes the form of an asset transferred by the third party, the deduction for the employer's contribution cannot exceed the amount chargeable on the employee. The above rules do not apply to contributions

Budget Summary

under retirement benefit, personal pension, or accident benefit schemes or to the new statutory corporation tax deduction for providing share-related benefits through employee schemes.

Anti-avoidance

Under current rules for Revenue-approved Company Share Option Plans (CSOPs), gains from share options exercised within three years of grant attract liability to tax but not to National Insurance Contributions (NICs); in addition, the tax is not collectible via the PAYE system. From 9 April 2003, both NICs and PAYE will be applied to such gains, though not so as to affect employees who exercise early for genuine reasons such as injury, disability, redundancy or retirement.

Gains from share options generally were brought within the scope of NICs in April 1999, but options granted before 6 April 1999 were excluded. This exclusion has apparently been exploited by artificial arrangements to 'pay cash bonuses through such pre-April 1999 options, followed by a series of partial exercises of the option'. From 10 April 2003, all such exercises are brought within the charge to NICs.

From 16 April 2003 for tax purposes, and from a date to be appointed (after Royal Assent to Finance Act 2003) for NICs purposes, it is proposed to introduce new measures designed to ensure that artificial transactions which increase or decrease the value of shares awarded to employees will be taken into account in computing the chargeable amount. Certain existing avoidance rules concerning 'dependent subsidiaries' will be scrapped as a result. From the same dates, the rules for taxing remuneration paid in shares and securities via unapproved schemes are to be widened to cover a broader range of financial products.

From a date to be appointed (after Royal Assent to Finance Act 2003), there will be changes to the existing tax and NICs treatment of employee shares that are subject to restrictions, conditions or conversion rights. These changes are intended to simplify the treatment and produce a fairer charge.

Reporting requirements for unapproved schemes are to be strengthened and made more consistent.

Employee Share Schemes

As announced in the Pre-Budget Report in November 2002, it is proposed to introduce a statutory corporation tax deduction for the cost of providing shares for employee share schemes where the employees are taxable in respect of shares acquired or would be taxable were it not for the fact that the scheme is Revenue-approved. Draft legislation was published on 19 December 2002. The new relief will apply in respect of shares acquired by employees in accounting periods beginning on or after 1 January 2003. The deduction will normally be based on the market value of the shares, at the time they are awarded or the share option is exercised (whichever is applicable), less any employee contribution given in respect of the shares. It will be restricted by any relief given in earlier accounting periods, in respect of the same shares, under pre-existing rules. Certain reliefs for shares provided under approved share incentive plans take priority over the new relief.

Simplifying Employee Share Schemes

1. Until now, the exercise of an option granted under a Revenue-approved Company Share Option Plan (CSOP) has not had tax-exempt status if it took place within three years of an earlier tax-exempt exercise under a CSOP scheme. With effect from 9 April 2003, this rule is to be abolished.

2. Also from 9 April 2003, CSOP options exercised within three years of grant but by reason of injury, disability, redundancy or retirement will not lose their tax-exempt and NIC-exempt status.

3. From that same date:

    • arrangements, within the rules of a CSOP scheme, for funding the exercise price and dealing with payment of PAYE and NICs will be acceptable to the Revenue as long as they do not give a right to receive cash;

- CSOP rules will be allowed to specify 'market value' by reference to published prices on recognised investment exchanges in terms similar to those for shares listed on the London Stock Exchange and on Wall Street; and

- the process for approval of schemes by the Revenue is to be improved, so that approval will normally be effective from the moment the scheme is established.

4. From the date of Royal Assent to Finance Act 2003:

- the definition of 'material interest' in the CSOP legislation is to be brought into line with the definition in the legislation for SAYE option schemes and approved Share Incentive Plans (SIPs);

- changes to SAYE and CSOP schemes will not have to be notified to the Revenue unless they are to 'key features';

- an employee will have the right to exercise a SAYE option where he leaves his job as a result of injury, disability, redundancy or retirement following a move between associated companies after a take-over or restructuring;

- the required holding period for shares within a SIP acquired by reinvestment of dividends will be brought into line with that applicable for SIP shares generally;

- other changes to the SIP legislation will be made to provide greater flexibility, particularly in relation to partnership shares.

5. Where tax is due under PAYE on the exercise of an unapproved share option and the employer is unable to recover it from payments due to the employee, the latter must make good the amount to the employer within 30 days of exercising the option. From 9 April 2003 for tax purposes, and from a date to be appointed (after Royal Assent to Finance Act 2003) for NICs purposes, this time limit is being extended to 90 days and the NICs rules aligned with the income tax rules.

6. The existing limit on the amount of NICs an employer may recover each month from an employee is being abolished and the period over which recovery may be made extended.

STAMP DUTY

Stamp Duty

Several measures are to be introduced to counter stamp duty avoidance, reduce the burden on smaller businesses and modernise the administration of the tax for individuals. The measures for transactions completed on or after 1 December 2003 where the transactions relate to contracts entered into after Royal Assent to the Finance Bill include the following.

- The existing charge applying to leases will be replaced with a single 1% charge on the net present value (NPV) of rental payments where the NPV exceeds the zero-rate band of £60,000 for residential property or £150,000 for non-residential property (see below).

- The stamp duty zero-rate band threshold for non-residential property will be increased from £60,000 to £150,000. This will also apply to non-residential new leases where the NPV of rents is not more than £150,000.

- Property purchases by individuals funded through alternative financing arrangements are to be put on a level footing for stamp duty purposes with purchases funded through conventional mortgages.

- Stamp duty is to be abolished on transactions involving property other than land, shares and interests in partnerships.

Budget Summary

From 10 April 2003, stamp duty will no longer be payable on certain non-residential property transactions in disadvantaged areas. The Inland Revenue has published a Statement of Practice SP1/2003 which sets out detailed guidance on the relief.

With immediate effect (changes generally applying to documents executed after 14 April 2003) a number of changes to the group and acquisition relief clawback provisions are to be introduced including:

- extending the period in which the clawbacks can be withdrawn to three years;

- closing a loophole whereby the clawback could have been avoided by transferring the land into a connected company before selling the original company together with the connected company; and

- ensuring the relief will be withdrawn unless stamp duty has been paid on the market value of land that is subsequently reacquired by the original company.

Stamp Duty on Short-term Tenancy Agreements

A new stamp duty exemption will apply where Registered Social Landlords (RSLs), such as housing associations, have entered into short-term tenancy agreements under contracts with local authorities to house the homeless.

The measure will retrospectively exempt from stamp duty such agreements entered into since 1 January 2000.

VAT

VAT Registration and Deregistration Limits

With effect from 10 April 2003, the VAT registration limit will be increased from £55,000 to £56,000. The deregistration limit will be increased from £53,000 to £54,000. The registration and deregistration limits for acquisitions from other EC countries are also increased from £55,000 to £56,000.

Incentive Scheme to Encourage Registration

From 10 April until 30 September 2003, as a one-off exercise, businesses trading over the VAT threshold but which have failed to register for VAT will be allowed to notify their liability to register outside the statutory time limits without incurring a late notification penalty provided they

- pay any arrears of VAT in full; and

- furnish all returns and payments on time for the twelve months after registration.

Continuous Supplies

With effect from 1 August 2003, the VAT Regulations will be amended to alter the rules governing the tax point for certain ongoing (or continuous) supplies between connected businesses. At present, the tax point rules for these supplies mean that VAT becomes due only when a VAT invoice is issued or a payment is received, whichever is earlier. Some businesses have exploited these rules for the benefit of connected businesses that cannot recover all of their input tax by delaying (sometimes indefinitely) both payment and invoicing. Where such supplies are made between connected businesses, the new regulation will ensure that tax points will be created periodically, in most cases based on 12-month periods, to ensure that accounting for VAT cannot be 'indefinitely or excessively delayed'.

Flat Rate Scheme

With effect from 10 April 2003, the scope of the flat rate scheme will be extended by increasing the turnover ceilings. The VAT-exclusive annual taxable turnover ceiling will be increased from £100,000 to £150,000, and the total turnover ceiling will be increased from £125,000 to £187,500. A new table of trade sectors will be introduced on 1 May 2003. This will introduce three changes to the trade sectors ('mining and quarrying', 'journalism' and 'hairdressing or other beauty treatment services') and will provide better definitions of the two building sectors.

VAT Car Fuel Scale Charges

The scale used to charge VAT on fuel used for private motoring in business cars will be increased from the start of the first accounting period beginning on or after 1 May 2003. The revised scale charges are as follows.

Annual returns

Cylinder capacity of vehicle	Scale charge diesel £	VAT due per car £	Scale charge petrol £	VAT due per car £
1,400 cc or less	900	134.04	950	141.48
1,401 cc to 2,000 cc	900	134.04	1,200	178.72
2,001 cc or more	1,135	169.04	1,770	263.61

Quarterly returns

Cylinder capacity of vehicle	Scale charge diesel £	VAT due per car £	Scale charge petrol £	VAT due per car £
1,400 cc or less	225	33.51	237	35.29
1,401 cc to 2,000 cc	225	33.51	300	44.68
2001 cc or more	283	42.14	442	65.82

Monthly returns

Cylinder capacity of vehicle	Scale charge diesel £	VAT due per car £	Scale charge petrol £	VAT due per car £
1,400 cc or less	75	11.17	79	11.76
1,401 cc to 2,000 cc	75	11.17	100	14.89
2,001 cc or more	94	14.00	147	21.89

Simplified Import VAT Accounting

With effect from 1 December 2003, approved importers will be able to provide reduced, and in some cases zero, security in relation to the import VAT element required under the Duty Deferment Scheme. Importers will need to seek approval from Customs. Details of the approval criteria are the subject of continuing consultation with the trade and will be published in due course.

Evidence for Input Tax Deduction

With effect from 16 April 2003, where businesses that operate in trade sectors dealing in

- computers,
- telephones (and their respective related equipment),
- alcohol products, and
- oils held out as road fuel (including those buying fuel in such quantities that the fuel is kept in storage other than the fuel tanks of vehicles)

Budget Summary

seek to recover VAT without a valid VAT invoice, they will be required to provide a higher standard of evidence to be entitled to input tax deduction. This will include evidence of the *bona fide* nature of the transaction.

Customs will not apply the measure until a limited consultation has been carried out but, thereafter, if they identify a business in one of the affected sectors holding an invalid VAT invoice, the measure will be applied to supplies made on or after 16 April 2003.

Annual Accounting Scheme for Small Businesses

The annual accounting scheme allows businesses with a taxable turnover of up to £600,000 to make one VAT return a year instead of the usual four. With effect from 10 April 2003, businesses with a taxable turnover up to £150,000 (previously £100,000) may join the annual accounting scheme immediately. Other qualifying businesses must have been registered for twelve months (no change).

VAT on Sales of Freehold Commercial Buildings

VATA 1994 and the VAT Regulations 1995 will be amended with effect from Budget Day, to block a scheme which has been used to avoid VAT on most of the sale price of a new freehold commercial building. The scheme took advantage of VAT Regulations, reg 84(2), which allows VAT to be declared when payment is received, rather than at the date of sale. The scheme involved the use of contrived transactions with uncertain prices, and involved delaying paying the bulk of the consideration until after three years, when the payments could be treated as exempt by virtue of VATA 1994, s 96(10A). This provision will be amended so that the liability of payments made after three years will remain standard-rated. The new legislation will also block avoidance schemes involving the sale of vacant land and the subsequent construction of a commercial building.

Business Gifts Relief

With effect from 1 October 2003, VATA 1994, Sch 4 para 5 will be amended to bring the VAT treatment of a series or succession of gifts into line with the VAT treatment of an individual gift. No output tax will be due provided that the total cost of gifts made to the same person does not exceed £50 in any twelve-month period. However, output tax will be due in full on all the gifts if the total cost exceeds £50.

Face Value Vouchers

The Government is to make significant changes to the VAT treatment of face value vouchers (such as gift vouchers or telephone cards). VATA 1994, Sch 6 para 5 is to be repealed, and new legislation is to be introduced, with effect from 9 April 2003.

Currently, when face value vouchers are sold, there is no VAT payable on the transaction at the time of sale, except to the extent (if any) that the consideration exceeds the face value of the voucher. VAT is only due when the vouchers are redeemed for goods or services. The issuer who redeems the voucher accounts for VAT only on the amount for which the voucher was initially sold, irrespective of the value which it is redeemed for. Any trading in face value vouchers by intermediate suppliers has been disregarded for VAT purposes.

The new legislation will restrict this treatment of face value vouchers to sellers who both issue the voucher and take on the obligation to accept the voucher in return for goods and services which they supply. Any intermediate suppliers who sell vouchers will be liable to account for VAT on the full amount for which they sell a voucher. The VAT will be due when the voucher is sold. Intermediate suppliers will be entitled to recover input tax on their purchase of such vouchers, subject to the usual rules. Where it is known that the face value voucher had been redeemed for zero-rated goods or services, the intermediate supplier may make an adjustment to reflect this (but will have to adjust input tax as well as output tax).

There will be some exceptions to this general rule. Where a face value voucher is sold as part of a package or similar composite transaction, and the price of the package is not adjustable if the consumer were to refuse the voucher, the voucher will be treated as supplied for no consideration and a delay in accounting for VAT will not be appropriate. In addition, the treatment of face value vouchers that have been issued by an issuer who does not itself redeem the voucher, but where the redeemer accounts for VAT on the full face value, will remain unchanged. Sales of postage stamps at or below face value will continue to be disregarded for VAT purposes.

Supplies of Electronic Services from Outside the EU

The EC VAT on E-Commerce Directive amends the EU rules governing the place of supply of electronically supplied services with effect from 1 July 2003. These rules are being implemented separately in the UK. Services supplied by non-EU businesses to private individuals and non-business organisations in the EU will be taxed in the country where the customer belongs. The changes mean that non-EU businesses that provide such services to EU customers could be required to register and account for VAT in every EU Member State where they make supplies. However, the UK has confirmed that it will introduce a special scheme allowing such businesses to register electronically in a single Member State of their choice, and declare the EU tax due on a single electronic VAT return to the Member State of registration (which will then distribute the VAT due to the appropriate Member States).

Exchange of Information with other EU Countries

With effect from the date of Royal Assent, existing legislation empowering the UK tax authorities to assist other EU countries in ensuring compliance with tax legislation and countering fraud will be consolidated. In addition, a new power to amend references to European legislation by statutory instrument is being taken to provide the flexibility to accommodate future changes to EU legislation.

Joint and Several Liability

With effect from 10 April 2003, a new measure will be introduced to tackle VAT 'missing trader' fraud. Subject to a series of safeguards, it will make businesses in a supply chain jointly and severally liable for tax that has not been paid by a missing trader. Where a business receives a supply of specified goods or services in circumstances where it knew, or had reasonable grounds to suspect, that VAT on those goods or services would go unpaid, it will be held liable for the tax due if the supplier defaults on payment. Initially, the measure will be restricted to telephones (including telephone parts and accessories) and computer equipment (including parts, accessories and software).

Customs: Civil Penalties

Customs are to introduce two types of civil penalty for businesses and individuals who import or export goods to or from countries outside the EU, and fail to meet their legal requirements under Community and national customs law. There will be two types of penalty: a 'penalty for non-compliance' and an 'evasion penalty'. Penalties for non-compliance may be imposed in cases of 'occasional serious error' involving at least £10,000 duty and/or VAT; persistent failure to comply with regulatory obligations (including low level errors in declarations); and failure to correct deficiencies in systems, operations or physical security when directed by Customs. The maximum penalty will be £2,500. Evasion penalties may be imposed as an alternative to criminal prosecution. The maximum penalty will be an amount equal to the duty and/or VAT sought to be evaded, but the penalty may be reduced to take account of co-operation. More serious cases of evasion will continue to be dealt with by prosecution. The necessary legislation will be included in the 2003 Finance Bill, and the new penalties will come into effect in the autumn of 2003.

Security for VAT

With effect from 10 April 2003, Customs' powers to require security where they consider that a business represents 'a direct risk to the collection of VAT' will be extended. VATA 1994, Sch 11 para 4 will be amended. The new provisions are intended to affect businesses 'which, despite warning, continue to deal with other businesses or individuals that evade paying tax' by deliberately using VAT registration numbers belonging to other businesses without their knowledge; by going missing; or by becoming insolvent while owing VAT. It may also affect those that trade with such businesses. The aim

Budget Summary

of the new proposal is 'to tackle serious cases of VAT evasion where several businesses act together to attack the VAT system'. The new provisions will allow for a proportionate security requirement from each business, in order to protect the total tax at risk in a VAT supply chain.

Anti-avoidance: Property used for Private or Non-business Purposes

From 9 April 2003, businesses which purchase land and buildings to be used partly for business and partly for private or other non-business purposes cannot use the 'Lennartz' approach as a way of paying VAT on the private use. Any private and non-business use of land and buildings must be dealt with by apportionment of the VAT incurred at time of purchase so that only the business element is treated as input tax and recoverable. (Under the 'Lennartz' approach, businesses are allowed full input tax deduction on the purchase of an asset and subsequently account for private use by an output tax charge arising over the lifetime of the asset. Because buildings depreciate very slowly and can be disposed of exempt from VAT, this provides an opportunity to delay or avoid payment of VAT.)

TAXES ON EXPENDITURE

Tobacco Duties

With effect from 6pm on 9 April 2003, the rates of duty on tobacco products imported into, or manufactured in, the UK are increased by 2.8% in line with inflation.

Alcohol Duties

With effect from midnight on 13 April 2003, the duty on beer and still wine is increased in line with inflation, adding 1p (duty and VAT) to a pint of beer and to a standard 175ml glass of wine. The excise duty on spirits, cider and sparkling wine is frozen.

The reduced rates scheme for small breweries remains unchanged, except that calculations of duty liability must now be based on the new standard beer duty rate of £12.22 per hectolitre per cent abv.

Vehicle Excise Duty

Following the introduction of graduated vehicle excise duty for cars, the Budget 2003 introduces a new rate of VED to provide an incentive for the use of cleaner cars. The most environmentally friendly cars (with carbon dioxide (CO_2) emissions below 100g/km) will now pay £55 per annum, while the most polluting vehicles (those that produce CO_2 emissions of 186g/km or more) will now pay up to £165. VED for lorries and motorcycles will be frozen.

Amusement Machine Licence Duty

The current rates of amusement machine licence duty remain unchanged.

Gaming Duty

With effect for accounting periods starting on or after 1 April 2003, the gross gaming yield (GGY) threshold for each duty band will be increased as follows.

First £502,500 of GGY	2.5%
Next £1,115,500 of GGY	12.5%
Next £1,115,500 of GGY	20%
Next £1,953,000 of GGY	30%
Remainder	40%

General Betting Duty

The Government is making a number of changes to General Betting Duty. For accounting periods beginning on or after 1 June 2003, betting exchanges will pay duty on the revenue which they receive for controlling and facilitating betting (i.e. their commission) at a rate of 15%. For accounting periods beginning on or after 1 September 2003, bookmakers and pool promoters will be allowed to carry forward losses. For bets made on or after 1 September 2003, the duty exemption for on-course bets will only apply to bets made at horserace and dog tracks.

Insurance Premium Tax: Protected Cell Companies and Higher Rate IPT

Some types of motor insurance and domestic appliance insurance are liable to higher rate IPT at 17.5% when sold by a supplier of cars or domestic appliances, or by persons 'connected' to such a supplier. Insurance sold by a person who is not 'connected' is liable to IPT at the standard rate. With effect from the date of Royal Assent, the definition of 'connected persons' will be extended to include, in certain circumstances,

- protected cell companies;

- companies with a similar cellular structure; and

- those who use such companies to sell the types of insurance that are liable to higher rate IPT.

Reform of Bingo Duty

With effect from 4 August 2003, the duty on the stakes paid by players and the duty on money added to prize funds by bingo clubs ('added prize money') will be abolished and replaced, subject to exemptions, with a duty on the bingo promoters' gross profits at the rate of 15%.

Air Passenger Duty

The rate of APD is frozen in the light of heightened global uncertainty.

ENVIRONMENT AND RESOURCES

Landfill Tax Increase

The standard rate of landfill tax has been increased from £13 per tonne to £14 per tonne with effect from 1 April 2003. It will rise again to £15 per tonne next year.

Climate Change Levy

There are a number of changes to climate change levy. The Finance Act 2000 will be amended to exempt products used in secondary recycling processes that are not eligible for either the existing 'dual use' or 'non-fuel use' exemption, but which compete with primary processes that are eligible for that exemption. The products in question have been exempted by extra-statutory concession since July 2002.

The Finance Act 2000 will also be amended to provide for the introduction of a formal mechanism whereby relief claimed by the operator of a combined heat and power station, using data relating to the previous year, can be reconciled against the station's actual performance during that year of operation.

There will be further amendments to Finance Act 2000 to require suppliers to account to Customs for the levy at the end of every 'relevant averaging period' where its exempt supplies exceed the amount of qualifying electricity purchased or generated. (The relevant obligation currently only applies to a supplier who ceases making exempt supplies of renewable source electricity.) This change will apply to averaging periods ending on or after 31 March 2003.

Aggregates Levy

The rate of aggregates levy is frozen at £1.60 per tonne.